SAMonNOW – Orlando

A practical approach to
Software Asset Management
on the ServiceNOW platform.

Software Asset Management in 3 phases
Visibility, Agility & Accountability

Orlando Version June 2020

Bill L. Cypert

SAMonNOW
Stop Wasting Software Asset Management $$$

ISBN 9798652127855

Dedication

This book is primarily dedicated to the center of the greatest love story of my life. She <u>melts me</u>. <u>every</u>. <u>time</u>. I see her. (Even though sometimes it is with a screaming child in her arms.). Without her constant encouragement this book would not have been written.

She is my best friend. Szeretlek Orsolya!

This book is also dedicated to the great men and women in the trenches of IT everyday. We strive to do more than just "keep the lights on" by thinking (and taking action) strategically on behalf of our organizations.

When a recurring theme started to emerge among my customers about the best ways to get started with ServiceNow Software Asset Management (SAM) the idea for this book was born. I searched everywhere for a solid resource on the topic. When I could not find much, I decided to write a book on the topic.

My hope is that you will find a nugget or two to move your SAM efforts forward. If you find anything and surely you will, that should be improved / corrected in this book, please let me know so I can get your updates in the next version.

Bill Cypert
bill@billcypert.com

Page Intentionally left blank to preserve
section layout.

www.billcypert.com

Table of Contents

Section 4 Agility Phase

Section 7 Supporting Materials

Disclaimer

The views expressed throughout this book are strictly mine and should not be construed as those of any organization nor my previous employer ServiceNow.

Additionally, as ServiceNow is publicly traded and this book primarily is focused on best practices in leveraging one of their products, you should not take this book, nor any comments therein as my endorsement of their stock although in full disclosure I am a ServiceNow stockholder.

The intent of this book is solely to educate organizations on best practices when implementing Software Asset Management on the ServiceNow platform, specifically the Orlando version of the product.

Preface

This purpose of this book is to provide an effective introduction to and roadmap for Software Asset Management (SAM) implementations leveraging ServiceNow, specifically the Orlando version. It would be impossible to address every SAM scenario as these are driven by different factors at each organization.

This book should be used as a guideline in terms of procedures in the Software Asset Management space. Your organization can leverage this information as an outline in creating and refining your own SAM process. The bottom line is that your process needs to be owned by you and your organization based on best practices.

Wherever possible, I have tried to stay "out of the box" as possible in terms of ServiceNow Platform and the ServiceNow SAM Professional Module. The release of this book is in line with the Orlando release of ServiceNow.

Assumptions

1 – SAM is installed & activated.*
2 – SAM roles are active.*
3 – You have reviewed and have a basic understanding of the SAM dashboards.*

*More information about each of these assumptions is included in the pre-reqs (chapter 2) and in the supporting materials section (chapter 7).

Advice on Consuming this Book

This book has three primary sections.

Introduction. Sections 1 & 2 are intended to provide an answer to the question of Why software asset management is important and an overview of SAM on the ServiceNow platform.

Process Phases. Sections 3 – 6 provide detailed information on implementing SN SAM in your instance.

Supporting Materials. Section 7 provides reference materials such as Project Success, Organizational Change Management, Setting up SAM, SAM Dashboards Explained and a Glossary of Related Terms.

Page Intentionally left blank to preserve
section layout.

www.billcypert.com

Section 1 – Why Software Asset Management

Page Intentionally left blank to preserve
section layout.

www.billcypert.com

Introduction

Recently I got a text from my wife asking why we were paying for both Spotify and Amazon Prime Music, two services with completely redundant offerings. "We're not", I said plainly and somewhat smugly. "I switched to Amazon Prime and cancelled Spotify months ago."

Yeah…turns out I'd forgotten to cancel Spotify and as a result we'd been paying for both services for five months. Of course, I wasn't even using Spotify, but I was paying for it regardless. After scraping the egg from my face and going through the Spotify cancellation process, I had the situation back under control. It was a silly oversight that left us five months of Spotify service poorer.

Why am I telling you this story? Imagine that my Spotify account was a software license and I was a large enterprise. Instead of one Spotify account I have hundreds or thousands of them. Alongside these I have hundreds of installed seats for dozens of other software packages, each with its own terms of service, licensing periods, and usage requirements. I'm just one guy using a simple music service and I couldn't properly keep tabs on my billing overlap. Imagine this on an enterprise scale. The potential gotchas grow exponentially, as do the potential costs and the amount of information you need to track and keep current with.

My absentmindedness regarding my Spotify account cost me five months of service I didn't use. That's chump change in the grand scheme of one person's life.

But for a company with a multitude of dense license agreements and software deployments the potential losses and overspending can be much higher, and there can be severe consequences for companies using software that isn't properly licensed.

This is where Software Asset Management (SAM) comes in. SAM systems are designed to help companies of all sizes keep current on all the moving parts surrounding their software licenses. SAM makes certain that you're properly following all of the specifics in your license agreements for all of the software your company uses. Apart from all of the headaches, both literal and figurative that this saves you there are a number of benefits companies derive from properly implemented SAM systems.

Photo by Zhen Hu on Unsplash

Software spending is brought under control

Companies of any size have an existing license base representing the total number of legitimate software licenses they own. Generally, the larger the company the larger the existing base. If you aren't tracking where these licenses are being used, or if they're being used at all you may be overbuying new licenses when new computer systems are purchased, or currents systems need to start running existing software. Older computers are often repurposed or retired and the software licenses they were using are no longer needed. Because SAM makes the location and usage status of all your licenses fully transparent, you're able to redeploy those existing licenses onto new machines saving a good deal of money over purchasing new licenses.

Photo by KS KYUNG on Unsplash

When companies aren't certain where their software packages are deployed and whether they own enough licenses to cover them they'll often drastically over-purchase licenses to protect themselves. This sort of wasteful spending can be eliminated entirely with a well-designed SAM system that tells you exactly how many licenses you have and how many you need. For larger companies the cost savings can be significant.

Additionally, a deep understanding of how software is being used in your organization allows you to explore eliminating unused software or switching to free or less expensive alternatives. You can also eliminate maintenance contracts on software that no longer requires them. This can often be a considerable savings.

Software license risk is curtailed

When you're working with dozens of software packages, each with its own license term lengths and renewal periods the possibility of inadvertently falling out of compliance is high when a renewal is missed. This can be a significant problem if a lapse in license coverage happens to coincide with an audit of your organization's compliance. SAM systems keep tabs on all of your licensing windows and alert you when renewals come due.

SAM can also identify software packages with potentially unresolvable licensing issues that could wind up being security or compliance problems, and that could cost you quite a bit of additional IT support resources. This foreknowledge gives you the option of cutting ties with the offending software before any major problems develop.

Photo by Micaela Parente on Unsplash

Photo by Micheile Henderson on Unsplash

Auditing costs are dramatically reduced

If you're keeping tabs on your software license usage with a manual system or worse, not keeping track of it at all you can be caught badly off guard if a software licensing watchdog group becomes aware of your activities. The resulting audit could turn up serious problems, which can result in large fines and other unplanned costs associated with bringing all of your existing software licenses into compliance.

Using a properly executed SAM system prevents this sort of fiscal shock by making all of your current license deployments fully transparent and traceable.

On top of that consider that many companies conduct their own internal audits on a periodic basis in order to make certain they're in compliance. This helps take the sting out of official audits, but these internal audits impose their own time and financial costs, many of which can be eliminated with real-time software asset management. With SAM you'll know whether you're in compliance at all times, rendering any sort of audit far less necessary.

The fact is that software licensing represents a major liability exposure for any company that employs even a moderate amount of commercial software. And with the software industry and their watchdog groups stepping up efforts to snuff out licensing abuses the need to properly ensure full compliance at all times has never been higher.

Even if you are in compliance there is often a lot of waste that goes into and results from maintaining it. SAM systems certainly bear exploring if you're currently falling victim to any of the negative scenarios we talked about above. The money and headaches they can save you make them well worth the look.

Page Intentionally left blank to preserve
section layout.

www.billcypert.com

A few weekends ago, I was "resting" between sets something major dawned on me. It wasn't Wimbledon or Roland-Garros, this was the much more competitive ATL people with day jobs league. We all wish we could move around the court like deities Roger and Serena but we live down on Earth at the 4.0 USTA level. So there I was, out of breath looking at my shoes (Adidas Barricades btw, not NIKE not that there is anything wrong with that), then asked the CIO I was playing if he knew about the 2018 Nike vs Quest court case. He said no and the idea for this and the next chapter were born.

In the introduction we looked at the fundamental Software Asset Management (SAM) concepts and explained how SAM systems can help protect companies against licensing contract infringements and limit their potential liability. Now let's examine how this operates in the real world.

On April 24, 2018, Quest Software brought suit against sportswear giant Nike claiming massive licensing shortfalls, and use of illegal, pirated software keys. The lawsuit seeks just over $15.5 million in damages - damages Quest says are due after performing an extensive audit on Nike's license usage.

Of course, the merits of the case still need to be decided, but it presents us an interesting opportunity to explore software asset management in a real-world context. This is the first of two chapters on the lawsuit and SAM systems. In this one I'll discuss SAM from the plaintiff's perspective, looking at how software asset management could have mitigated many, if not all, of the alleged infractions before they ever became problematic. In the second we'll hop over to the defense table and see how SAM systems could have made proving Nike's counter-case much easier.

Let's take a look at each of the major infractions Quest is claiming against Nike and how proper software asset management could have prevented these from becoming an issue.

Copyright Infringement

Quest is accusing Nike of having far too few purchased licenses to support the number of machines running the software and the number of additional potential users that have been given access to the software on remote machines.

This is the most frequent infraction in a software audit, and Quest is building a name for itself as a company that aggressively audits their customers looking for these sorts of shortfalls. Without having a proper SAM system in place it's very difficult to keep track of hundreds or thousands of licenses and this sort of situation is common. This is why software asset management is so important. If Nike had been keeping proper tabs on all of their software licenses in a disciplined, automated manner there would have been little chance that software licenses could have gone unaccounted.

Breach of Contract

After Quest's audit was complete and they confronted Nike with the $15.5 million-dollar figure, Nike refused to pay and countered with a significantly lower amount. Quest took this refusal to pay as a breach of the contract Nike originally signed with the software company. This was, in Quest's opinion, a separate matter from the original infringement.

Again, if Nike had been using proper software asset management practices there wouldn't have been any new information revealed during Quest's audit, if the audit had taken place at all. With adequate SAM protections in place Nike would have been able to account for all of their current Quest software installations.

It's likely that many of the violations Quest found were caused by improper re-harvesting of license keys from defunct, retired, or repurposed machines. We also know that Nike had a number of freeware and trialware copies of Quest software installed. All of these incomplete keys can show up in Quest's audit as unlicensed, improperly versioned, or potentially illegal. This could have distorted Quest's numbers and made Nike look more culpable than it really is.

Proper SAM protections would have helped head these violations off before they caused problems. Proper re-harvesting of keys and correct interpretations of freeware licensing requirements would have freed up existing keys for other machines and assured a clean audit, free of improperly designated illegal installations.

Digital Millennium Copyright Act (DMCA) Violations

The DMCA disallows any technological interventions intended to circumvent copyright protections. Quest asserts that Nike did this by using illegally-obtained, pirated license keys to access Quest software. Nike vehemently denies this charge.

It's likely that this wasn't a regular Nike practice, but instead the result of rogue employees. Had Nike been using adequate software asset management measures, these employee behaviors would have been discovered long before they became a problem for the company because their installations wouldn't have been included in the SAM software's list of allowed installations.

Potential Users vs. Actual Users

One of the most contentious elements of Quest's lawsuit is their claim that Nike is allowing large numbers of devices POTENTIAL access to Quest software. It's not clear that these devices ever actually use the software. Only that they have access to servers that contain Quest software that could be used.

What's at issue are competing interpretations of key clauses in the Software Licensing and Support Agreement both parties signed. Quest feels that any potential user needs to be an authorized user while Nike disagrees, contending that only actual users need to be authorized and that they shouldn't be charged for "access-adjacent" users.

As before these charges could have been avoided had Nike been using a SAM system. SAM systems help assure that all proper precautions are being taken to ensure compliance with all current licensing agreements. With internal company watchdogs keeping tabs on user behaviors, someone likely would have raised a question about this "access-adjacent" practice before it ever lit up signals on Quest's radar.

Summary

Had Nike been using proper SAM protocols it's unlikely that Quest would have had reason to conduct their audit in the first place but had they anyway they wouldn't have found the level of abuse they're alleging. Nike would have been able to demonstrate, with certainty, the validity of their installations and the presence of the requisite number of license keys to account for their installed base. They would have had a proper understanding of their SLSA agreement in its entirety, avoiding improper and potentially damaging interpretations of key clauses. In general, Nike's exposure would have been greatly reduced had they had adequate software asset management systems in place.

In the next chapter we'll look at this suit and Nike's countersuit from Nike's perspective. It's their contention that very few of the alleged abuses actually occurred and that Quest's audit was predatory and overreaching. We'll discuss how proper SAM systems would make proving their case significantly easier.

The key take away of this chapter is that If you are ever in the greater Calgary area or at Knowledge the next time we have one without Covid, then bring your racquet and lets hit some fuzzy yellow balls. Ok, the real key takeaway is that you should strongly consider if you want to be the next NIKE with a Quest all over you or if you want to chat about Software Asset Management best practices. Seriously though, message me for tennis or prescriptive guidance on the ServiceNow platform be it SAM, ITOM, PPM or my Agile/OCM approach to large projects.

Page Intentionally left blank to preserve
section layout.

www.billcypert.com

1.3 Nike countersues Quest (May 2018)

If you've skipped to this chapter and you haven't already read chapter one you'd do well to go back a few pages and read it first. To summarize, Quest Software is suing Nike for copyright infringement, breach of contract and DMCA violations stemming from an audit Quest conducted to determine Nike's licensing status.

Quest is seeking $15.5 million in damages. Nike refused this amount but did agree they owed Quest roughly $350,000 for actual violations. Nike, on May 31st of this year countersued Quest, alleging predatory and inaccurate auditing practices on the part of the software company. In this chapter we will look at how proper software asset management practices could have helped Nike make its case.

Predatory Auditing Practices

I mentioned in the last chapter how Quest Software has been steadily building its auditing program over the last several years and has become quite a formidable force, with the number of audits it performs increasing year after year. What's not clear is whether this is in answer to a truly rampant licensing problem or that it's a growth industry for the company, using strong-arm auditing tactics to fleece customers for money. With their countersuit Nike seems to be contending the latter.

And potentially for good reason. The inclusion of potential, but not actual users of Quest software represents a large portion of the bill presented to Nike. If Nike is to make their case that $350,000, instead of $15.5 million is the proper amount they owe they'll need to demonstrate that these potential devices don't represent a usership that requires licensing.

How might proper software asset management practices have been employed to help Nike defend itself? To begin with, Nike should have made itself aware of exactly what Quest was looking for, how its auditing scripts handled the search, and where this search was being performed. It appears that Quest was given full access to Nike's servers without any controls at all.

The difference between Quest's and Nike's audit was the basic definition of "user". Quest's audit counted any person or device that came into proximity of Quest software as a user by default, even if they never actually used the software. Nike restricted their search to actual users of the software. This difference in definition accounts for a massive disparity between the amounts each side feels is owed.

Nike should have had an audit defense in place prior to any audit being performed. They should have been aware of the different ways auditing scripts could define usership and been prepared to dictate search terms. It would appear that Nike didn't take advantage of the negotiation phase prior to the audit. Here they could have set ground rules, and these ground rules could have been guided by proper SAM systems. Nike did perform their own audit, but only after the fact. This self-audit will be pivotal in their defense and in the prosecution of their countersuit, but had it been performed routinely prior to Quest's audit it could have been used to help define baseline restrictions on Quest's audit.

Photo by Alexander Daoud from Pexels

Freeware and Trial Licenses

Quest's audit also turned up a number of software installations they deemed unauthorized because they used freeware or trialware licenses that Quest, understandably, didn't pay for. Nike's defending itself by saying that their SLSA agreement with Quest did not expressly forbid the use of these sorts of software licenses and that because Quest did specifically add this restriction into agreements it had with other companies, this omission represented a tacit acknowledgement that freeware and trialware licenses were acceptable.

Had Nike been performing self-audits on a regular basis and had been using well-policed SAM procedures there would have been an active and accurate accounting of all of these licenses. Nike could have used this information during the negotiation phase of Quest's audit to clarify search parameters. They also could have used this information when reviewing their SLSA agreement to be certain their behavior was covered under the terms of the contract before any suits were filed.

Keeping Tabs on Current License Usage

It's important to note that Nike isn't denying they had compliance issues. Their counteroffer of $350,000 to cover the licensing shortfalls their internal audit uncovered is evidence of a modicum of good faith. And the fact that they gave Quest's auditors full access to their systems without any restrictions on the search parameters seems a good indication that they didn't think they were guilty of any major violations. However, had Nike been using proper software asset management procedures even the shortfalls they acknowledge could have been avoided. And the records that these systems would have generated would have gone a long way toward establishing compliance in the face of a prospective Quest audit.

Making Their Case

Certainly, Nike will use their own audit as the substantive basis for their claim that "unauthorized" users should be defined specifically as people actively using the software without a license, as opposed to non-users that simply had access to software but didn't actually take advantage. They'll use this data to support their argument that Quest's predatory auditing techniques, and the resulting shortfalls they report, represent a bad faith claim against Nike, and that they're only entitled to restitution for actual, not imagined potential deployment overages.

In the end a properly designed and maintained software asset management system could have avoided many of the issues Quest cited in their audit. The audit may never have taken place if Nike had its own data to present at the inception of their talks. SAM represents a good faith attempt to the companies you purchase software from, to be transparent and upfront about your software usage. It demonstrates that you take the issue seriously. I suspect Quest would have been far more likely to accept the $350,000 Nike offered them to make up for the shortfalls they found if they'd had that information available from the beginning.

Of course, if you take a skeptical view of the entire situation it is possible to see Quest as the sole villain, using unfair and deceptive auditing practices to milk unsuspecting companies for cash. If this is the case then there was likely nothing Nike could have done to prevent Quest's audit, regardless of how thorough their software asset management practices were. Predators will predate regardless of how prepared their prey is. But had Nike been ready with their own well-founded numbers from the beginning they would have had a strong case in their defense at the onset of litigation.

It will be very interesting to follow this case to its conclusion. Depending on what the outcome is the world of software asset management could be impacted permanently.

Section 2 – SAM on NOW Overview

Page Intentionally left blank to preserve
section layout.

www.billcypert.com

2.1 SN SAM Introduction

Leveraging the ServiceNow single platform for Software Asset Management allows you to transition to a proactive approach rather than the traditional reactive one most companies endure. Ingestion of software information is easy with ServiceNow, but one of the best features is the automated reconciliation engine. This engine provides up to date compliance positions for software publishers that are conveniently viewable on comprehensive dashboards.

Actual and potential issues trigger alerts that keep you always informed. Once alerts are received the remediation of non-compliant software can be automated. The two most common remediation automations used by organizations are software purchasing and revocation. This decision is made easier by the visibility provided by the SAM dashboards revealing current positioning.

ServiceNow provides visibility into each of the eight stages of the Software Asset Lifecycle. Please refer to the graphic on the next page and the subsequent short descriptions of each phase.

We must remember that Software Asset Management is heavily tied to many other processes within your organization.

Here is a non-exhaustive list to get you thinking ahead:

Application Portfolio Management (APM)
Catalog (Service Catalog)
Change Management
Contract Management
Cost Management
Fulfillment of Requests
Hardware Asset Management (HAM)
Procurement

2.2 SN SAM Pre-Requisites

I appreciate all of the kind responses to my first book on Software Asset Management on ServiceNow. Many people suggested adding in a pre-requisite section, so here it is.

1) Identify your internal subject matter experts
    a. Application Owners
    b. Application Admins
    c. Deployment Admins
    d. Related Technical Resources
   Note: This is partial list for a more complete picture, please refer to the "Primary Roles in SAM" section of this book.
2) Identify all software entitlements
3) Data sources you expect or would like to integrate with SAM
4) Request and activate SAM plug-ins (see next section)

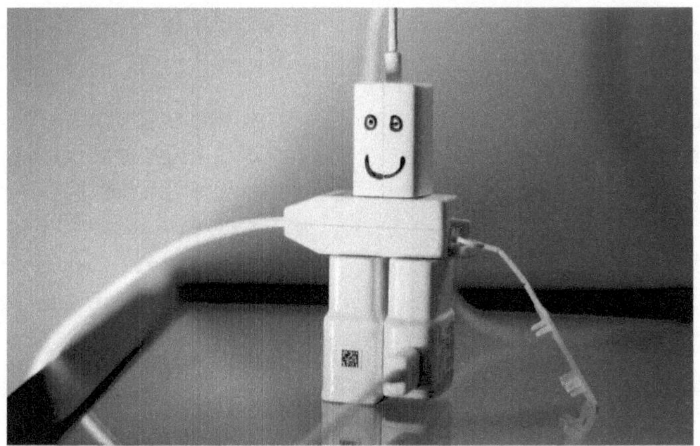

Photo by **Steve Johnson** from **Pexels**

SN SAM Plug-ins

Functionality on the ServiceNow platform can be dramatically increased by leveraging plugins. As I am sure you are aware, plugins are typically deployed to achieve specific outcomes via features & functionalities.

Here are a few different ways you may choose to add plugins to your instance.

- Built in plugins with the base out-of-the-box (OOB) ServiceNow instance

- Admin activated plug-ins

- ServiceNow activated plug-ins. In this case you must submit a Hi ticket to request the plug-in(s) activation in your instance. This is most often the option when the given plugin is tied to a subscribed to service such as SAM. Described later in this section.

BE CAREFUL: After a plugin is active, you cannot disable or deactivate it.

In the case of SAM as with other platform adds, there are multiple plug-ins needed and they have dependencies on each other. The good news is that in most cases ServiceNow will tell you about the dependencies prior to activating the plug-in. Generally, you can accept and have all of the plug-ins activated together.

Plug-in Activation for SN activated plug-ins*

1. Go to **[HI] > Service Catalog**.
2. Choose **Request Plugin Activation** - https://hi.service-now.com/hisp?id=hisp_sc_item&sys_id=891f08 8e465667e234a3cb52ffa1d299
   - **[Required]** In **Target Instance**, select the instance on which to activate the plugin.
   - **[Required]** In **Plugin Name**, enter the name of the plugin to activate.
   - **Note**: Plugins are activated in two batches each business day in the Pacific time zone, once in the morning and once in the evening. If the plugin must be activated at a specific time, enter the request in the **Reason/Comments**. Date and time must be at least 2 business days from the current time. Please provide a business justification in the Reason/Comments section and Customer Support will expedite the request as necessary.
   - **[Optional]** In Reason/Comments, provide any information that would be helpful for the ServiceNow personnel activating the plugin. For example, if you need the plugin activated at a specific time

instead of during one of the default activation windows.

3. Click **Submit**.

Activate a Plugin*

Customers can activate most plugins on their non-production instance, otherwise, they will have to request to get that plugin activated via the Now Support (HI). Some features require a separate subscription from the rest of the ServiceNow Platform. Some plugins require a purchased subscription before activation. Some plugins must be activated by ServiceNow Customer Support.

For evaluation, you can activate the plugin for an application that requires a purchased subscription on a non-production instance. To activate the plugin on production instances, you must purchase the subscription. To purchase a subscription, contact your ServiceNow account manager.

Activating a Plugin*

1. Navigate to **System Definition > Plugins**.
2. Find and click the plugin name.
3. On the **System Plugin** form, review the plugin details and then click the **Activate/Upgrade** related link.

   If the plugin depends on other plugins, these plugins are listed along with their activation status.

   If the plugin has optional features that depend on other plugins, those plugins are listed under Some files will not be loaded because these plugins are inactive. The optional features are not installed until the listed plugins are installed (before or after the installation of the current plugin).

4. (Optional) If available, select the **Load demo data** check box.

   Some plugins include demo data—Sample records that are designed to illustrate plugin features for common use cases. Loading demo data is a good practice when you first activate the plugin on a development or test instance.

   You can also load demo data after the plugin is activated by clicking the Load Demo Data Only related link on the System Plugin form.

5. Click **Activate**.

Activating a plugin included in your Subscription*

For Production instance, you can activate plugins that are provided with your subscription(s) using your Subscription Management module using the following steps:

1. Access the instance as admin
2. Go to Subscription Management
3. Click on Subscriptions
4. Select one of the related Subscriptions
5. Under Subscription Applications, click on the related Product. There you will see the related plugins and their status being (Active/ inactive).
6. Click on the desired plugin and click on Activate/ repair.

*Information pulled directly from ServiceNow KB0695388.

2.3 SAM Lifecycle Stages

Often people define Software Asset Management as "the process and infrastructure to effectively manage, control and protect software assets during all stages of their life."

Although some individuals may think differently, assets, specifically software assets do not just appear and disappear at random. We must make put forth our level best to fully track assets from before they enter our organization to until their ultimate disposal.

It is very important that everyone involved in a SAM project from individual contributors to key stakeholders fully understand this lifecycle. Once we examine the lifecycle in detail, we can begin to make a plan. As they say the most important part of a executing a plan is coming up with one in the first place.

Once we have our plan, then we can iterate as needed to improve our plan. It never ceases to amaze me how many organizations for which I consult that do not truly understand where they stand. However, they do know things need to get better and often have an end goal in mind.

This is why the best place to start is with understanding of the whole lifecycle and you currently work within it. Then you can do a GAP Analysis to determine what you need to do.

Software Asset Lifecycle

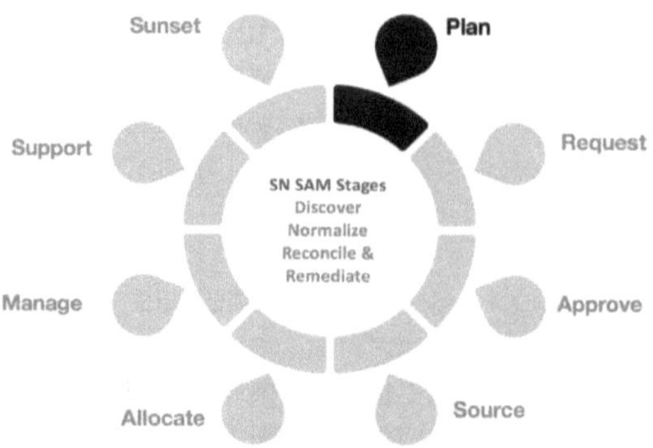

2.3.1 SAM Lifecycle Stage 1 – Plan

Planning is the key to success with Software Asset Management. This stage includes defining the operating framework, ensuring that you have executive and peer sponsorship throughout the organization, a solid communication plan and the appropriate tools to keep everything & everyone on the same page.

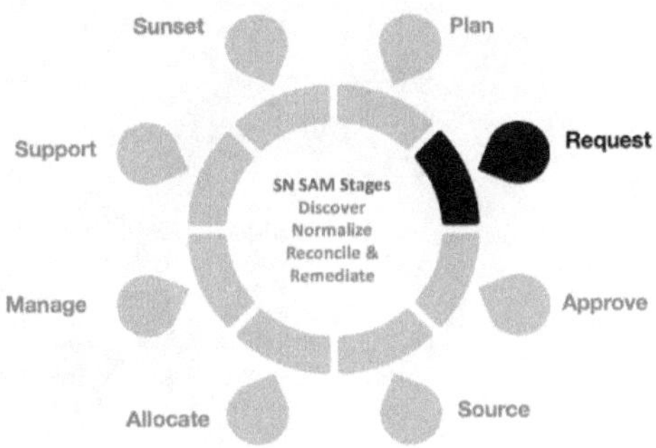

2.3.2 SAM Lifecycle
Stage 2 – Request

Request of software should be handled via the Service Catalog. Ensuring ordering through this singular vehicle helps not only identify the software needs of the organization but also us to standardize the process & software being ordered.

Obviously, we would build catalog items for all standard software. If we do not have a catalog item for a given software, then this would signify the need for greater scrutiny & approvals.

47

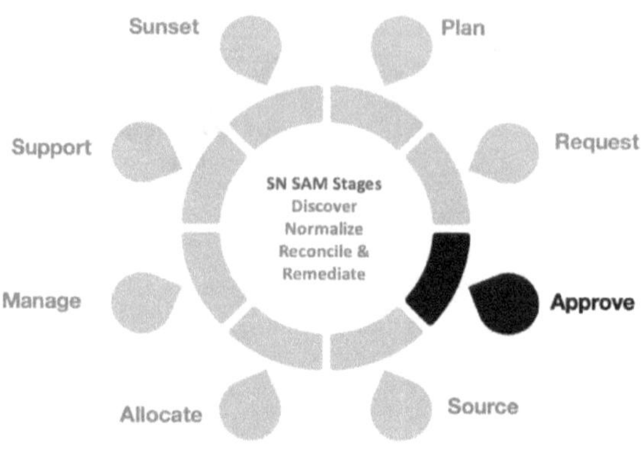

2.3.3 SAM Lifecycle
Stage 3 – Approve

All software requests should go through some level of approvals. Depending on the impact to the organization some software will only require the requestors manager, whereas in other situations it may require C-Level approval (think of something breaching an Oracle contract position).

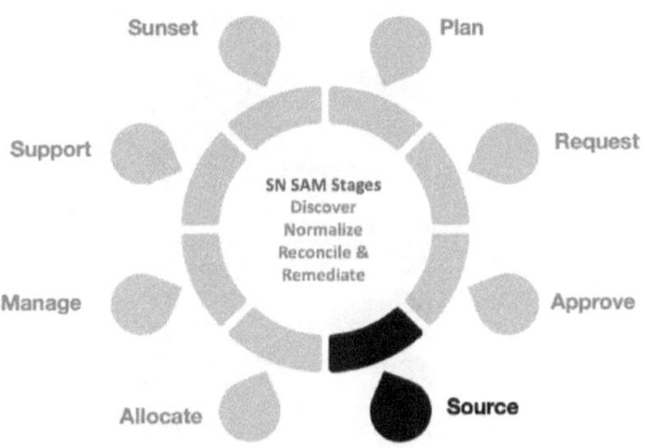

2.3.4 SAM Lifecycle Stage 4 – Source

Although most people think of the source stage as the purchasing stage, in many if not most cases, it is utilization of current inventory as opposed to a new purchase. In a mature organization inventory levels would be checked, then if needed additional inventory would be secured. This is often a stage that gets organizations in trouble or at least in a wasteful situation as people order software on an individual or department level without understanding the organizations current inventory position.

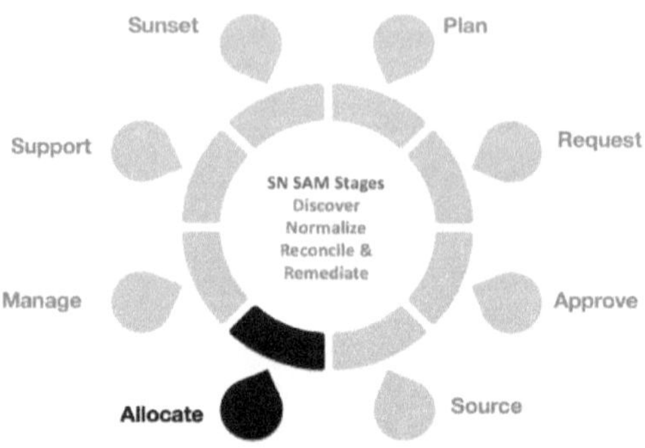

2.3.5 SAM Lifecycle
Stage 5 – Allocate

Allocation and tracking thereof yields tremendous savings to a company. Often I see organizations "over-allocated" and at the same time "under-allocated" by the same software vendor. Although this may seem understandable with silos it speaks to the need for a centralized Software Asset Dashboard.

As my coach in college used to say "the scoreboard doesn't lie".

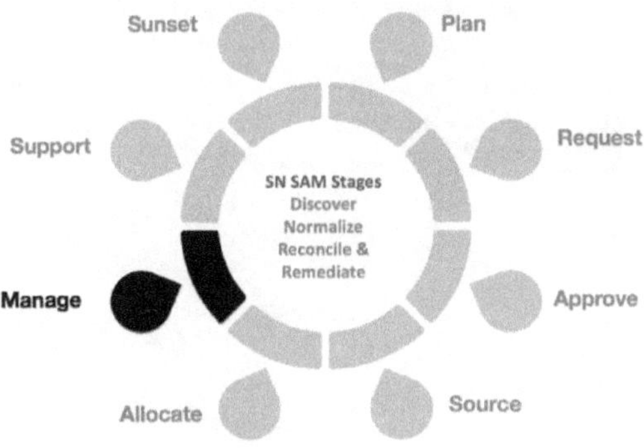

2.3.6 SAM Lifecycle
Stage 6 – Manage

Discovery, normalization, reconciliation and remediation are all typically considered part of an ongoing SAM program. Configuration management and Software management are pulled together in this stage as this is all about what the organization is currently using.

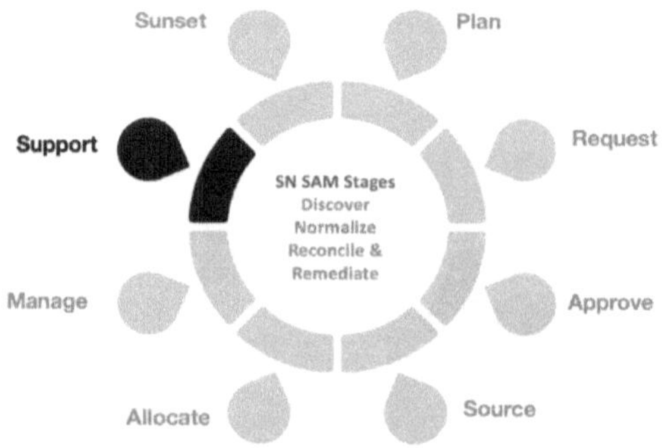

2.3.7 SAM Lifecycle
Stage 7 – Support

Support in the SAM sense is typically related to upgrades and their potential impact on our current disposition in terms of software allocations. There are several considerations regarding running multiple levels of similar software in a production environment. In most cases it is recommended to test the impact of upgrades with the dev & test environments prior to pushing these changes to production, even if the new version does not require additional funding.

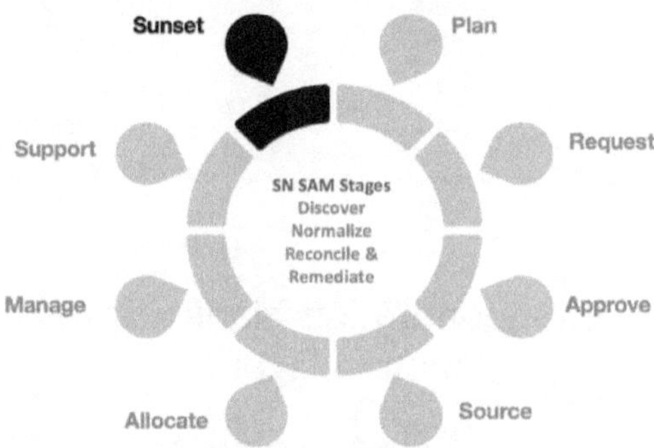

2.3.8 SAM Lifecycle Stage 8 – Sunset

Sunsetting is the EoL or End of Life of a given software product. This stage is critical from multiple perspectives such as security and accounting. There are many horror stories regarding improper disposal of EoL software and it's subsequent negative impact on the organization.

Page Intentionally left blank to preserve
section layout.

www.billcypert.com

2.4 SAM Program Goal

One of the primary program goals when implementing SAM is to reduce (or eliminate) IT waste in the form of unneeded software expense. This includes closely monitoring ownership, allocation, utilization, full life cycle and disposal of the IT Software related assets.

In thinking about the goal of Reducing (or eliminating) unneeded IT software expense, we can break this into three smaller focus areas.

Maintaining compliance

Optimizing spend

Supporting software audits

This section of the book will start at high-level strategic objectives then quickly move to tactical best practices. Although your application of these principles and specific steps will be unique to your organization, please remember that they are proven across many customer environments. Therefore, I strongly suggest you try to stay as close to the spirit of this plan as possible. As I pointed out before, it leverages OOB (out-of-box) whenever possible, so should be less hassle when it comes time to upgrade.

Page Intentionally left blank to preserve
section layout.

www.billcypert.com

2.5 Program Objectives (Top 10)

"Here are my 10 Commandments for SAM, well actually these should be considered 10 strong suggestions"

These are not in a particular order and may differ at your organization. However, my experience is that most organizations implement SAM programs to address most if not all of these ten objectives.

1| Enhance compliance posture in defense of software related audits.

2| Reduce pointless software purchases by fulfilling purchase requests with existing software inventory

3| Capture and track all purchased software entitlements within the organization

4| Track allocation and utilization across the entire organization including satellite locations and also contractors

5| Reduce spend through application rationalization which leverages utilization to determine duplication of solutions

Photo by Magda Ehlers from Pexels

6| Consolidation of reporting to enhance purchasing leverage. Buying at the organization level in opposition to the department or individual level.

7| Identifying "rouge" software on the network which has not been allocated through the appropriate SAM model.

8| Reduce or eliminate the need for antiquated human interrogation techniques when measuring allocation and utilization.

9| Report on purchased but not deployed, recycled, unallocated, beyond support and other software key indicators.

10| Provide visibility to organization and supporting teams such as change management, support and patching teams, etc.

Photo by Severin Höin on Unsplash

2.6 Guiding Principles

In an effort to provide you prescriptive guidance for your overall SAM effort, here are a group of "guiding principles" you should consider putting in your Standard Operating Procedures (SOP). Obviously these need to be taken with a grain of salt considering your specific organizational goals, policies and principles.

Photo by Joël de Vriend on Unsplash

2.6.1 Principle 1

The SAM SOP shall be the single source truth regarding SAM policy and procedure decisions within our organization.

> **Justification:** Adherence to this principle yields one consistently predictable procedure across all organizational units and locations.

Photo by rupixen.com on Unsplash

2.6.2 Principle 2

Purchases, allocations, entitlements, installations, removals and destructions shall be recorded and updated in the IT Asset Repository.

> **Justification:** The IT Asset Repository is only as good as the information recorded in it. It must be accurate and up to date to provide value to the organization.

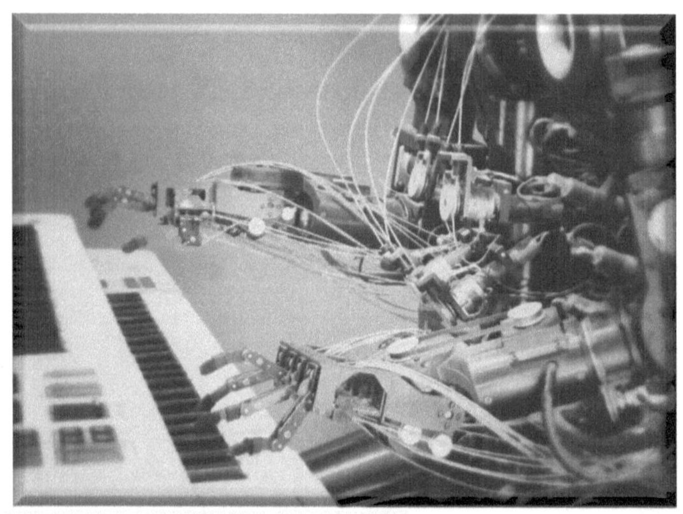

Photo by Franck V. on Unsplash

2.6.3 Principle 3

Automate software status (installation, allocation, utilization, deprecation, etc.) data collection whenever possible.

> **Justification:** Leveraging tools designed to perform automation of repeatable tasks improves accuracy and decreases cost as humans are freed to perform higher level tasks.

Photo by Jose Fontano on Unsplash

2.6.4 Principle 4

Access control must be enforced regarding SAM data. Rights should only be granted to individuals requiring access as a direct part of completing the organizational objectives for SAM.

> **Justification:** Changes must be approved and determined to be in line with the vision of the program as interpreted by the SAM process owner.

Photo by Scott Graham on Unsplash

2.6.5 Principle 5

Accountability for the entire process is ultimately the responsibility of the SAM process owner including policies, procedures and other direction/interpretation of the SAM process.

> **Justification:** Consistency and accountability for the SAM process is best when there is one overall owner. This yields more stability in process interpretation, execution, utilization of supporting tools for the entire organization.

Photo by Michelle Tresemer on Unsplash

2.6.6 Principle 6
End user software becomes a removal candidate if it has not been used in the previous 90 days.

> **Justification:** This allows reporting on harvestable licenses, which typically yield cost savings through better utilization.

Photo by Cytonn Photography on Unsplash

2.6.7 Principle 7
Software should only be installed with the express written consent of IT Operations.

> **Justification:** Requirement of consent typically reduces shadow IT installs, provides clarity to the organization regarding the approved software and enhances security auditing as clear definitions regarding approved allocations.

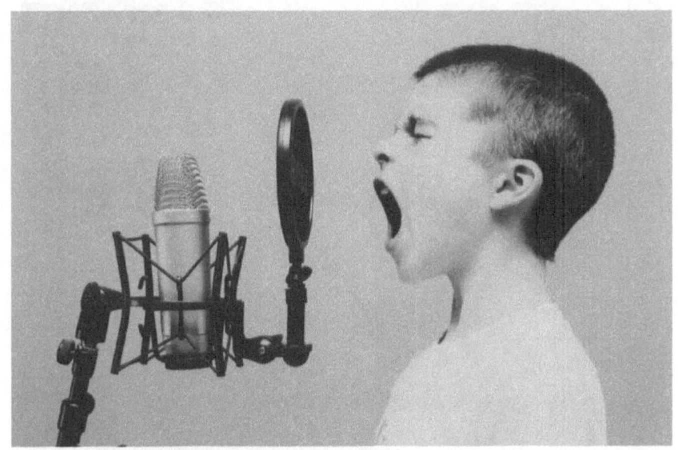

Photo by Jason Rosewell on Unsplash

2.6.8 Principle 8

Compliance of software licensing shall be reported on consistently to the internal and external stakeholders.

> **Justification:** What we inspect gets better, which is definitely true in this case. I have found that just putting in the appropriate visibility to the organization regarding asset allocation and utilization suddenly brings improvement.

Photo by Jason Dent on Unsplash

2.6.9 Principle 9
All software contracts shall be tied to their corresponding entitlements and maintained in a software contract repository.

> **Justification:** This allows for quick reconciliation between the contracts and the alerting conditions we link to each software asset.

Photo by Sharon McCutcheon on Unsplash

2.6.10 Principle 10
Software purchases should always be made from a central budget and if applicable shown or charged back to the ordering cost center.

> **Justification:** This increase to purchasing power, negotiation strength and also makes tracking much easier.

Page Intentionally left blank to preserve
section layout.

www.billcypert.com

2.7 Primary Roles in SAM

Depending on the size and structure of your organization, the following ten key roles for SAM may be filled by more or less than ten individuals. The importance here is that someone is taking responsibility in each of these areas. If ownership is not taken, then your SAM efforts will be severely hindered. SAM projects are never "complete" as they will always require care and feeding in the form of good procedural execution. The good news is that this becomes much easier if you set up your program properly.

Change Manager
CMDB Administrator
Contract Manager
Executive Sponsor
Procurement Manager
SAM Administrator
SAM Process Owner
Service Catalog Manager
Software Asset Manager
Stakeholder(s)

2.7.1 Change Manager

Ensures that an effective Change Management process is in place to control all changes within the infrastructure, including all changes to software.

- Ensures Requests for Change (RFC) information is accurate.

- Matching RFCs against affected Cis, obtained/stocked assets and available software entitlements.

- Verifying every scheduled change that happens.

Additionally, the Change Manager must ensure that Asset and Configuration Management are informed of any and all changes that are completed.

2.7.2 CMDB Administrator

Has the overall accountability for ensuring the suitability of the Configuration Management process to the organization.

- Ensures Configuration Management Data-Base (CMDB) is complete, compliant and correct.

- Report on changes of all CI's in the CMDB based on obtained/stocked assets and available software entitlements.

- Verify with internal audit the validity and correctness of all CMDB CI reports for Asset Management.

The CMDB is not supposed to be the biggest database, but rather the most accurate. If we want a good SAM program, we must have great control of our CMDB.

2.7.3 Contract Administrator

Demonstrates a strong attention to detail along with the ability to discover potential risks to the organization.

- Entitlement & license chief negotiator with vendors.

- Approves contract extensions, true-ups, and renewals for software licenses.

- Collects and maintains software contract license and support information in a central repository.

The Contract Administrator should analyze contracts looking for opportunities to reduce costs and increase profits, while ensuring compliance with the law.

2.7.4 Executive Sponsor

Sets the overall business vision for SAM and helps senior leadership understand the full business value.

- Ensures team focus on the realization of business value.

- Keeps SAM aligned to organizational strategy and goals.

- Provides timely resources and decisions to the SAM project.

Due to the problem-solving needs of the role the executive sponsor often needs to be able to exert pressure within the organization to overcome resistance to the project.

2.7.5 Procurement Manager

Ensures that the software procured is the correct quality, quantity, consumption model (time & place), and is purchased for the best price.

- Processing approved acquisition demands for software licenses and entitlements.

- Providing PO information for software entitlements to the SAM Administrator.

- Issuing PO's processed in a third-party application (e.g. ERP systems such as SAP).

- Providing contract-related data to the SAM Administrator for representation in the asset repository (e.g. software model retirements, changes to upgrade/downgrade terms and conditions)

To avoid over and under license situations often caused by "the tyranny of the urgent", the Procurement Manager must develop alerts to manage pro-actively.

2.7.6 SAM Administrator

Creates and maintains software asset data, including Software Models, Entitlements and Blacklists.

- Builds & shares SAM focused dashboards for organization.

- Provides the Software Asset Manager reports on compliance and completeness.

- Designs and deploys Software Discovery Models. Resolves partially matched and unmatched SD models.

- Conducts blacklist reconciliation for non-compliant software installations.
- Managing key relationships with peer roles within the enterprise.

The person in this role must be able to build consensus with peer roles throughout the organization.

2.7.7 SAM Process Owner

Responsibility for effectiveness and efficiency of the SAM processes. This person must ensure incremental improvement to actively applied every SAM process.

- Defining a compelling SAM process mission.

- Monitoring SAM process KPI's and targets.

- Reconciling when the SAM process when performance is out off target.

- Documenting and communicating mission, goals, and objectives to all process partners.

- Influencing proper staffing and preparing for process execution.

- Applying the Continuous Improvement Process (CIP) to the SAM process.

The person in this role must have the authority and inter-personal skills to ensure the SAM processes & procedures are established and followed consistently.

2.7.8 Service Catalog Manager

Achieving success as the Service Catalog Manager is most often measure in incident deflection and organization participation. In a SAM context, the Service Catalog manager must ensure that software requesters have an intuitive way to request software that is tied the procurement management flow.

- Publishes and removes software on behalf of the Software Asset Management group.

- Publishes a Service Catalog item to request software that does not exists in the current catalog. (to reduce shadow IT & document changing organization needs).

- Owns Service Catalog workflows and items related to Software Asset Management.

The person in this role must have the ability to empathize with the end users and thereby make ordering of catalog items as frictionless as possible. When I have seen good UX (User Experience), I have seen greater adoption.

2.7.9 Software Asset Manager

Maintaining strategic relationships with peer roles within an organization is the key to success for the Software Asset Manager. In this role the assigned person must be the "glue" that keeps everything together.

- Execution of the process is the daily role.

- Ensuring strong reporting across leading and trailing indicators.

- Escalating any issues with the process to the SAM Process Owner.

- Establishment of Change process in regards to any modification of the SAM processes.

- Reconciliation of discovered software installations vs viable license positions for each software publisher.

- Analyzing software utilization reports and setting up removal rules for software that isn't used frequently.

Remember, this is the primary "doer" role. Successful SAM deployments always a conscience effort to remove all obstacles for this person. I recommend daily stand-ups with this person for at least the first 6 months post go-live.

2.7.10 Stakeholder(s)

Interest parties in the Software & Hardware Asset information maintained in the CMDB and Asset modules.

- Feedback on current, future and previous state in regard to their area(s) of focus.

As with any project, there will be many stakeholders. Obviously, success in modern organizations is dependent on gaining consensus from many stakeholders. Therefore, where possible try to incorporate more visibility into potential stakeholders' areas of interest.

Page Intentionally left blank to preserve
section layout.

www.billcypert.com

Section 3 – Visibility Phase

Page Intentionally left blank to preserve
section layout.

www.billcypert.com

3.1 The Three Phased Approach

I love the old Steven Covey quote that we should begin with the end in mind. This is especially true when planning a comprehensive Software Asset Management program. The ultimate goal is one of accountability in terms of resource utilization. Getting to this level seems daunting but not if we break it down into bite size chunks. Hence the three-phase approach, each with sub-phases that ultimately lead us to our end goal.

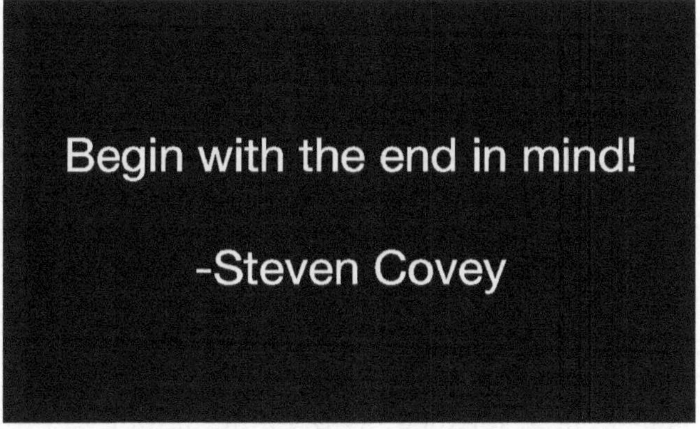

The three phases are Visibility, Agility and Accountability.

> **Visibility (Sect 3)** is basically figuring out what you have and who is using it.
>
> **Agility (Sect 4)** is how we care and feed for the SAM system, so that the information stays up to date.
>
> **Accountability (Sect 5)** is about security, audit and reporting inside and outside the organization.

These phases **should not** be viewed in a waterfall approach where you need to complete all of one stage prior to moving on to another. Quite the contrary as most organizations are in all 3 stages at once. As an example, my strong recommendation is to start with your "top" 2 software assets. Typically, this could be something like Microsoft and Adobe. The good news is by completing the Visibility stage for these two vendors, that you will be laying the groundwork for other vendors as the ServiceNow Discovery tool is same regardless of where you apply it. In focusing on just one or two pieces of low hanging fruit, you not only can demonstrate success to the organization in the form of early wins, but you also are establishing the framework for all of the other software assets that you will be taking through the three stages.

3.2 Visibility Phase Overview

The visibility stage is all about gaining an understanding of what you have today, what you are paying for and what you are actually using. Some organizations call this the baseline stage. Whatever you choose to call it, the bottom line is that you need to get a handle on where you are today.

Photo by Ali Yahya on Unsplash

Page Intentionally left blank to preserve
section layout.

www.billcypert.com

3.3 Initial High-Level SAM Plan

One of the biggest obstacles to successfully launching and running a SAM program, or many programs in business, is getting started. This is clearly a case where we can not let perfect be the enemy of good. Therefore the best way to start is to start.

Goal

To produce an <u>initial</u> Software Asset Management plan.

Timeline

< 1 Week. This is a 2 hour workshop followed by "chasing down" answers to questions that were not answered in the workshop.

Warning: Often organizations try to use building their initial plan as the time to improve/modify their processes. My experience is that this most often slows you down the project. Therefore I strongly recommend that you capture your current process today, with all its warts and look to change it later in the project.

Page Intentionally left blank to preserve
section layout.

www.billcypert.com

3.4 Visability Strategy

I personally like to walk through the "craddle to grave" for one common software title. Once we go through the steps below, then I typically have the organization "rinse and repeat" for at least 2 more software titles, so we are off to a good start.

This is not about boiling the ocean. We need a couple of the most common software applications to build our high-level plan. We do not want one off use cases as these are the exception not the rule.

Initial (aka high level) SAM plan can be broken into three "craddle to grave" steps. Each of these correspond to one of the 3 phases. Software order process is where we start as it is the begins our journey into Visability.

- **Software Order Process (Visability)**
- SAM Care & Feeding (Agility)
- Reclaimation / Removal / EoL (Accountability)

Page Intentionally left blank to preserve
section layout.

www.billcypert.com

3.5 Software Order Process

Typically when I work with customers, we gather representatives from separate business units for a white-board session.

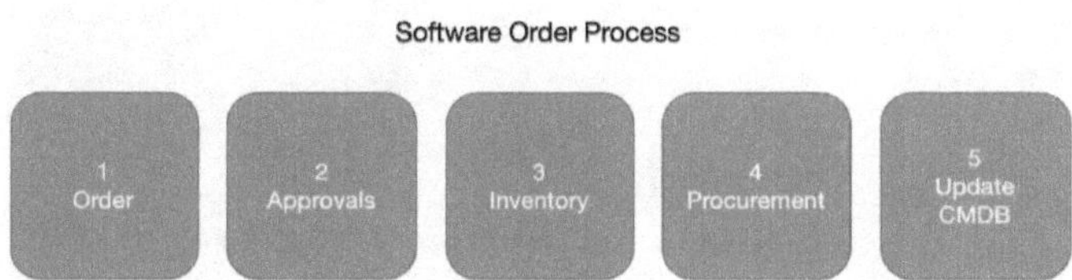

3.5.1 SOP Step 1 - Order

How does the typical non-IT worker order software in your organization?

In ServiceNow environments we often talk about providing end users with an Amazon like shopping expereince. I find it helpful to compare the Amazon experience with how things actually work with the organization with which I am consulting.

Have you ever called Amazon to help with ordering of an item or group of items? I personally have not. We are not talking AWS here, but rather Amazon, you know the retail giant.

How does this experience differ from your process of ordering software at work?

3.5.2 SOP Step 2 - Approvals

Who approves software purchases?

This is often contextual, such as manager or director. In ServiceNow we can "dot-walk" to reference fields on a related table based on the context of the individual requestor.

Some organizations have approvals of specific software also require additional approvers. This is most often done with software that is above a certain monatary threshhold such as $500 or where it may lead to compliance concerns.

Detail your approval process so we have it captured.

3.5.3 SOP Step 3 - Inventory

How do you check current inventory (aka entitlements) levels for the given software sku?

We do not want to be under or over on entitlements as both represent risk and waste to the organization.

Do we need to procure more licenses?

Have you ever bought something only to get home and realize you already own something similar? Imagine this scenario on a much larger scale within your organization.

Often siloed departs will own over entitlements to software while other departments are in the process of buying the exact software the organization already owns.

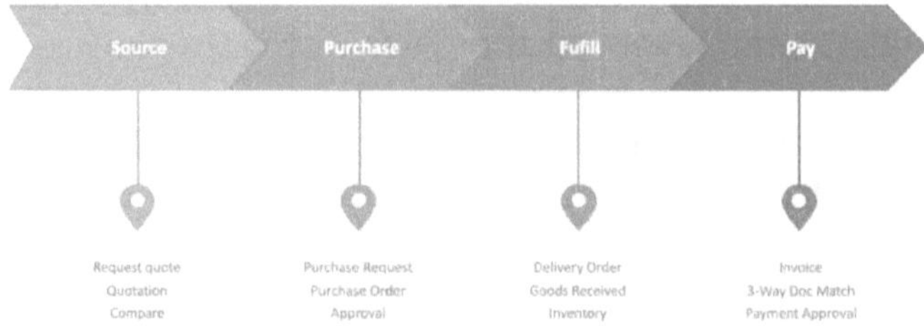

3.5.4 SOP Step 4 - Procurement

How are procurement decesions handled today for software? Do you leverage centralized budgeting or is it more ad hoc?

How does your current methodology compare to the typical 4 step procurement process?

Source
Purchase
Fufill
Pay

3.5.5 SOP Step 5 - Update CMDB

It is critical have a CMDB you trust that is acurate regarding your organizations software. In the CMDB context, we call these Configuration Items or CI's.

If you are like most of my clients early in a SAM deployment, you are probably rolling your eyes right now. We have all been told our whole careers about the importance of the CMDB to our organizations, but watched as CMDB projects fail time and again.

I have good news for you on the CMDB front. If you have a CMDB you trust then great! If you do not, then there are some things we can do that will get us through while we focus on SAM.

Page Intentionally left blank to preserve
section layout.

www.billcypert.com

3.6 Input Existing Software Data - Installs

Leverage the Software Asset Management Plan to perform an initial load of Software installation information from any reliable sources of information that the organization trust (including migrations from the **SAM Plugin**) into the Now Platform.

3.7 Input Existing Software Data - Entitlements

One of the initial steps to execute a SAM practice is to recognize what you have acquired to use in your environment. This is tracked as a Software Entitlement record. There are different sources for this data, for example, reseller reports and buy orders. The utilization of software entitlement data in reseller reports given by the company's software sellers to make/populate software entitlement records is the suggested practice. This is on the grounds that the software entitlement record in ServiceNow leverages a Publisher Part Number (PPN) and most companies don't have the PPN in hand at quick notice. The PPN is constantly incorporated into the reports that the software merchant gives to the publishers under the terms and conditions of their affiliate agreement.

Here is an explanation of the data we collect in this phase to upload into ServiceNow. Remember ServiceNow at its core is made up of records and data fields within those records. In this case we leverage MS Excel to format our input by labeling columns data fields and each row is an individual record.

Data Fields (Column Headers) Required		
Field	**Type**	**Description**
Publisher	General Value	Software Maker
Product	General Value	Title of Software purchased
Version	Text	Version of title purchased
Edition	General Value	Edition of title purchased
Purchased Rights	General Value	Purchase amount (# or qty)
Metric Group	List Choice	License metric
License Duration	List Choice	Perpetual or subscription based
Start Date	Date	Start of license consumption
End Date	Date	Start of license consumption

Data Fields (Column Headers) Not Required but very helpful		
Field	**Type**	**Description**
Publisher Part Num	General Value	Part number assign by manufacturer
Platform	List Choice	MS, Linux, etc.
Language	List Choice	English, Spanish, etc.
License Type	List Choice	Full, outright, upgraded, etc.
Unit Cost Currency	List Choice	Currency used to purchase software
PO Number	Text	Internal PO #
Unit Cost	Number	Cost for 1 unit
License Metric	List Choice	Compliance calculation
Asset Tag	General Value	Unique ID for asset
Owned By	General Value	Employee responsible for asset
Company	General Value	Owning company or subsidiary of asset
Location	General Value	Location of asset usage
Vendor	General Value	Seller of the asset
GL Account	General Value	General Ledger that reflects this asset
Cost Center	General Value	Cost Center purchasing this asset
Department	General Value	Department purchasing this asset

Page Intentionally left blank to preserve
section layout.

www.billcypert.com

3.8 Input Existing Software Data – Contract Info

Ensure that you capture all information possible regarding the existing software contracts. The importance here is around completeness and accuracy. In most cases if you can not find a given contract, then it is easiest to reach out directly to the appropriate vendor.

3.9 Input Existing Software Data – Usage Info

An initial ingestion of any and all usage information is extremely helpful. When we perform our initial audit we must compare that data against the usage information so that we can come up with a variance report. This variance report will be a form of guidance for the remediation of our environments.

Page Intentionally left blank to preserve
section layout.

www.billcypert.com

3.10 Perform Initial Audit

The initial audit is key to understanding where we stand in terms of our current software position in regard to usage, licensing, entitlements and other dispositions.

In the initial audit you must balance between speed and comprehensiveness. Remember this is the initial audit, therefore my rule of thumb is to do everything we can possibly do within a day or two max. In the past when I have left this open with customers, I have found that it usually goes one extreme or the other.

Either the customer does such a cursory audit that the information collected truly does not provide much value or conversely some customers get bogged down for weeks on the initial audit. This is another clear case for not letting perfect be the enemy of good. We need a decent amount of information, but we cannot get bogged down in the initial collection phase.

Therefore, I ask for customers to dedicate a day to this task and whatever the outcome is becomes the basis for our initial audit. If we are waiting on someone else, then maybe we give them a day or two to respond, but let's focus on getting what we can get and moving on.

Page Intentionally left blank to preserve
section layout.

www.billcypert.com

3.11 Software Publisher & Product ID

ServiceNow provides a growing PPN (Publisher Part Number) list. In most cases the software you ingest should be represented on this list. The software titles on this list will have an existing software model. However, it is not totally uncommon to have software that is not on the PPN List and therefore we do not have an automatic Software Model to referenced based on the PPN.

Therefore, at this point we must shift our focus to the additional step of creating a Custom Software Product record. The good news is that once we create this custom record, that we then can use it automatically in the future with matching software titles. In the next section we cover creating custom software product records.

NOTE: When we have software models that are subscription based like MS Office we will often have a PPN but not a software model. ServiceNow will create the software model for us and also a discovery map is also automatically populated.

Page Intentionally left blank to preserve
section layout.

www.billcypert.com

3.12 – Creation of Custom Software Product(s)

A Software Model is REQUIRED for all licensable software products! To create a software model, the following information is required: Publisher, Product and Product Type.

Key Point: We must ensure that we properly label subscription based software accordingly in the system. Also, we must add the Publisher as a new Company Record if the Publisher is not already listed in the SN Platform.

Photo by Kevin Bidwell from Pexels

Photo by fotografierende from Pexels

3.13 - Validation of Discovery Maps

Although   assignment is automated when a Software Model is created dependent on a software definition contained in the PPN Library, it is always best to validate the information is correct.

The Discovery Map is key to the mapping of the correct Software Model (and corresponding entitlements) when we run our reconciliation and discovered software is found.

Often if you took the step in 3.12 to create a custom software product then you will need to validate that the platform is suggesting the appropriate map. In most cases you will have a map available, assuming you entered everything properly in the custom creation step.

On the off chance that a substantial discovery map not accessible, then set up the conditions (e.g. version, edition, language, platform) and add these to the appropriate Discovery Model to ensure that the Software Model is correct.

3.14 Attribute Verification of Software Model

The next step is to validate the key attributes of the Software Model. This step consists of:

Blacklisting software as needed.

Marking on-premise or cloud-based location of software hosting.

Identifying if the software is part of a suite, is stand-alone or both.

Confirm correct discovery mapping on the Software Model. Obviously if this is incorrect, you must update this information immediately.

Validate the maximum installs is properly populated. This is key to correctly understanding our license positioning in future reports.

Page Intentionally left blank to preserve
section layout.

www.billcypert.com

3.15 Lifecycle Types

When there is a software lifecycle content for the Discovery Map, Lifecycle records are automatically created.

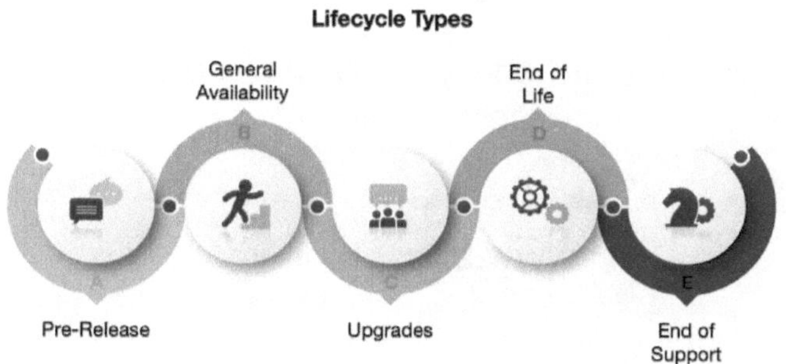

In the event that no lifecycle record is created automatically and a software lifecycle requires relation with the Software Model, generate the record and incorporate the proper lifecycle types (Publisher/Internal) and stages:

Pre-Release

General Availability

Upgrade

End of Life

End of Support (or Extended Support)

Page Intentionally left blank to preserve
section layout.

www.billcypert.com

Section 4 – Agility Phase

Page Intentionally left blank to preserve
section layout.

www.billcypert.com

4.1 Agility Phase Overview

The Agility Phase is about taking the baseline information you gathered in the Visibility Phase and now taking action on it or at least leveraging it to set good policies for your organization. It never ceases to amaze me that when we hit this stage people's behavior starts to change as now their actions become easily seen by the organization.

Remember the initial (aka high level) SAM plan is typically broken into three "craddle to grave" steps. Each of these correspond to one of the 3 phases. SAM Care & Feeding is the second step and is the focus of this section.

- Software Order Process (Visiability)
- **SAM Care & Feeding (Agility)**
- Reclaimation / Removal / EoL (Accountability)

Photo by John Cameron on Unsplash

Page Intentionally left blank to preserve
section layout.

www.billcypert.com

4.2 Request Software via Service Catalog

Start the demand for the Software Entitlement by utilizing the Service Catalog assuming you have already populated your Software Catalog Items. If not, then I recommend building a quick SC item for the software.

If you must use another method to keep going with you SAM build, then do so, but updating Service Catalog should be a high priority as part of any ServiceNow SAM initiative.

Photo by Peggy Anke on Unsplash

4.3 Software Request Approval

Assuming again that you are leveraging Service Catalog, then the approval process is very intuitive. I especially like the new swipe left and right functionality in the Madrid rebuild of the mobile application.

Note: Make sure that you log in with a mock user account and make several requests for software. Then log in as the appropriate approver and deny at least one request and also approve at least one. This way you can view what happens from the user, manager and SAM points-of-view in each case.

Photo by Marcus Aurelius from Pexels

4.4 Available Entitlement Verification

Figure out whether the software entitlement that is demanded is available and can be assigned to the client or device.

In the event that the entitlements are not readily accessible, start activities to decide how to obtain the entitlements.

Note: Does the system alert you if there are no available entitlements?

4.5 Validate Requirements for Software Acquisition

If you do not have the entitlements necessary to fulfill the software request and it has been approved, then the ServiceNow platform will generate a ServiceNow PO (SNPO) record in most cases. If you do not want to move forward with acquiring the software entitlement, then cancel the SNPO and go back and update the request status to denied.

If the SNPO is not automatically created, then you can manually create your own by providing as much as possible of the following information:

Vendor/Publisher

Number of required entitlement rights

License Metric

License Group

Stockroom

When the SNPO record is verified and finished, check with Software Asset Manager to ensure the record is accurate and that the software will be ordered.

If it is an open source or any type of software not requiring an additional purchase, then you may cancel the SNPO as generating a "real PO" will not be necessary. However some of my clients like to keep the SNPO for record keeping when updating all entitlements.

4.6 SNPO to Procurement Request

At this point, we have a SNPO for the software entitlement that has been demanded. However, at this point we only have record in ServiceNow and we need to interface with whatever our traditional mechanism is to create and approve a corresponding purchase order.

Therefore, once we approve the request in SN we now need to send this request over to the que of the organizational purchase order system so that a legitimate purchase order may be created, approved and fulfilled.

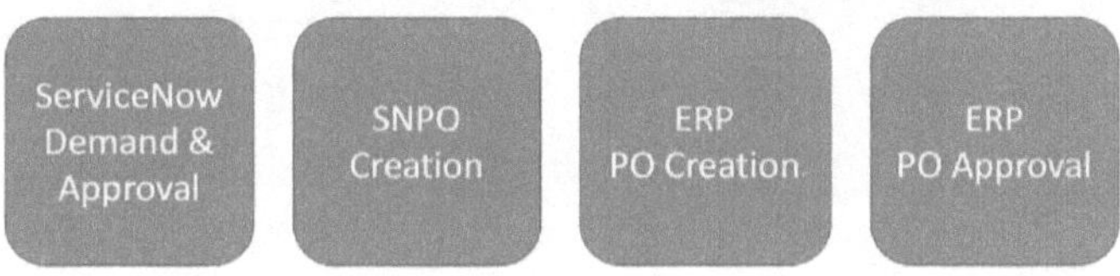

4.7 Create, Approve & Issue Purchase Order

On we receive notification from ServiceNow on the approved request for software, we must now create and subsequently approve a newly generated PO in our traditional external PO system.

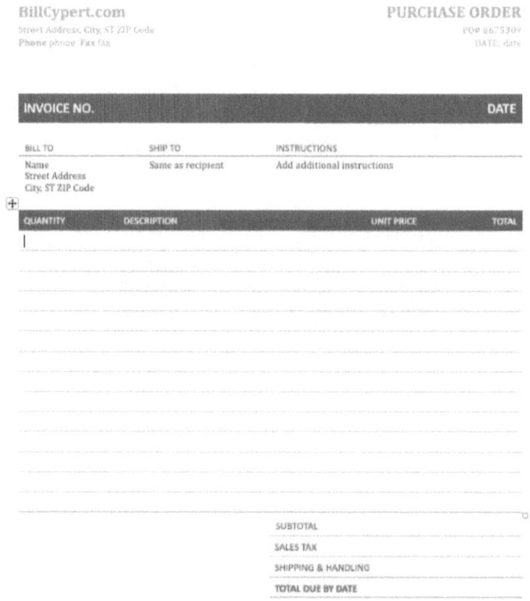

Now obviously we must Issue PO to appropriate vendor for fulfilment.

4.8 Update Procurement Request

Update attributes in the ServiceNow PO record accordingly after submission and approvals from the ERP with any and all appropriate information such as shipping details, etc.

4.9 Update Software Entitlement Information

Update software entitlement record in ServiceNow to reflect our new position. This should be a verification step as the system should reflect our new position and the SNPO should be closed. The operative word here is should, which is why we would be best served checking for ourselves to ensure accuracy of our records.

4.10 License Types & Software Models

Leverage the Publisher Part Number (PPN) Library for the following:

Publisher

Product

Version, Edition, Rev Level, etc.

Platform

Best Practice: ALWAYS leverage the PPN Library as it is constantly being updated and in most cases, it will pre-populate the appropriate Discovery Map corresponding to the chosen Software Model.

In the event that the software is accessible in the Publisher Part Number Library, yet an equivalent Software Model record can't be found, the software model automatically generated.

A Software Model Record can be manually created in the event that the product **isn't** accessible in the PPN Library. However, this is clearly a check twice cut once type of situation. I have on several occasions moved to fast and done a bunch of extra work rather than double checking if a PPN was available. Now the hard lessons learned I double and triple check prior to doing any custom inputs.

4.11 Upgrades and Entitlements

If you have an entitlement that includes upgrades to a new version of a software title, then ensure that you reflect the "new" license position in the SAM module.

However please keep in mind that in most cases this is not as simple as it may seem on the surface as typically, we go through rolling upgrade periods. This leaves us in the awkward position of maintain distinct software positions.

It can be a pain, but if you are diligent and work with IT to ensure proper cut off enforcement for support, then this is a doable task.

Software vendors have taken advantage of sloppy record keeping in the past to levy heavy fines for not understanding our positions in terms of upgrades & support. Therefore, I typically strongly recommend to IT that we set a firm cut-over date whenever possible to get us off the old software once the new software is tested and deemed to be ready for general release.

4.12 Metrics for Licensing

Document **Metric Group and License Metric** to ensure we are properly prepared for audit, reconciliation and reclamation efforts.

> **Metric Group Examples**: Adobe, Common, IBM, HP, VMware, Oracle, etc.

> **License Metric Examples**: Per Node, per user, per device, user CAL, device CAL, user subscription, etc.

4.13 Purchased Rights

Populate and/or update the appropriate number of entitlements that were purchased corresponding to the correct software title.

4.14 Connect Contracts & Entitlements

Ensure the all software contracts are added to the contract repository and also clearly connected to the appropriate license entitlements.

<u>This step is a must for Audit Defense!</u>

If the contract is not in the contract repository, then high priority should be given to getting it there and ensuring the entitlement count matches the contract.

4.15 Populate Entitlements with Financial Info

It is key to ensure that we capture all costs associated with software entitlements. Although this may seem as simple as looking at a Purchase Order and dividing by number of licenses, it is rarely so easy.

Software vendors are notorious for burying in cost that is not readily seen when only looking at POs. These could come in the form of support, upgrades, minimums and even maximums at given pricing levels. If you think back to our discussion on the NIKE vs Quest case, Nike is arguing that Quest is using these types of "predatory" practices.

I am not suggesting that I agree with NIKE's attorneys, but the fact that they can make such an argument shows that these types of situations are very real in our world today.

4.16 Upgrade and Downgrade Models

Many software contracts today are written so that the software is licensed in such a way that you may leverage current, past and/or future versions of the software. When this is the case you need to ensure that the Software Model related to the entitlement reflects this position.

This will ensure that once the primary version is authorized that the upgrade and downgraded software models will be appropriately account for during reconciliation.

Photo by Jukan Tateisi on Unsplash

4.17 Software Entitlement Record

In completing the Software Entitlement record, the following information should be updated:

> **Changes:** Upgrades, Downgrades, Cost Center, Department, Location

When the Software Entitlement is finished, check out the Software Model related to the entitlement record and decide whether any updates are required.

Often times you will find that you need to add additional attribute information especially in the case that the Software Model that wasn't being utilized before was created automatically. Remember this happens automatically when we select definitions in the PPN Library, but often the Software Model does not contain all of the info we need.

Page Intentionally left blank to preserve
section layout.

www.billcypert.com

Section 5 – Accountability Phase I

Page Intentionally left blank to preserve
section layout.

www.billcypert.com

5.1 Accountability I Phase Overview

The Accountability Phase is where we take the processes set in motion during the Agility & Visibility stages and now add in governance. Once we have our accountability in place, then things start to get much much better in the organization. We now clearly see rouge software, out of support as well as end-of-life titles. Additionally, and often overlooked is the new insight we have into utilization and the often-dramatic impact this has on software spend.

Remember the initial (aka high level) SAM plan is typically broken into three "craddle to grave" steps. Each of these correspond to one of the 3 phases. Reclaimation, removal & EoL (End of Life) make up the third step and are the focus of this section.

- Software Order Process (Visiability)
- SAM Care & Feeding (Agility)
- **Reclaimation/Removal/EoL (Accountability)**

Page Intentionally left blank to preserve
section layout.

www.billcypert.com

5.2 Assign Entitlements to Users (or Devices)

When we go through the process of granting entitlements to users, we must record this information so that we can keep track of who is controlling or assigned which resources.

We typically assign a slew of software assets to new hires. However not every organization keeps an updated accounting of the specific licenses that are tied to given users. Therefore, when a person changes responsibility or is terminated and no longer needs the same software entitlements it can be very difficult to reclaim these resources.

Remember in asset management we think about the big 3:

What? What is the software asset that is being assigned?

Where? Where is the software installed (i.e. laptop, server, kiosk, etc) and also where is this device on which it is installed physically located?

Who? Who is the user or group to which this software title is assigned?

Additionally, it is nice to have information such as Assigned Date, License Key, PO Data, etc.

5.3 Withdraw & Cancel Entitlement Rights

We typically withdraw entitlement rights for things such as:

> Suspensions / Terminations of Employee
> Removal / Refresh of Hardware
> Blacklisting Software due to Support
> EoL, Risk, etc.
> Underutilization of Entitlement

The withdraw of rights may be done on an individual basis or may be a corporate wide decision. If it is an organization wide removal then it is best to Cancel the entitlement rights completely. Update the subscription information in the Vendor License Portal.

5.4 Discover Installed Software

Typically, we run software discovery events daily to find software and the hardware devices on which it runs.

When we come across "new" information is pushed to the Content Curation Team so that they can ensure that it properly gets into the system. It is critical that we map these new findings in the SAM Central Data Service. This is the only way to keep our mappings up to date. Otherwise our info would quickly become stale.

5.5 Software User and Machine Validation

In the event that the Discovery system is returning data related with applications installed in a Citrix farm, verify user exists in sys.user table and the PC is represented as a CI record in the CMDB. However, in the event that user and PC records exist, continue to generate another software installation record or updating the current software installation with a time/date stamp.

5.6 Discovery Model Software Install Grouping

Software install records should be verified in the system or added accordingly. Take a look at areas where you can group based on similarity of **Publisher, Product** and/or **Version.**

This will allow you to go with similar Software Discovery Models which will dramaticaly improve your efficiency in the long run.

5.7   Software   Discovery   Models Normalization

The Software Content Library is constantly updated, ok well it is updated weekly, including normalization info such as:

Publisher

Version

Product Type

Platform

Language

Version / Patch Level

5.8 Remediate Unnormalized Models

In certain cases, we end up with Discovery Models that either cannot be normalized or where they are just incomplete. We need to remediate what we can to hopefully end up with a normalized publisher, but sometimes we end up only normalized partially or in a match not found situation.

Here are the 3 choices and a little information on each:

Publisher Normalized. We found a match that <u>includes all</u> the publisher and product information so can be validated.

Partially Normalized. Just as the name implies, this is the case where we have some of the needed information, but we are missing at least one key field.

Match Not Found. We set this attribute when we cannot find a valid match. This is usually homegrown software of a mis-key.

Regardless of which status is chosen, the information is passed on to the ServiceNow Content Curation Team via the SAM Content Service so that they can make decisions regarding organizational policies on which models to use.

5.9 De-activate Bad Normalized Software Models

When you come across Software normalization rules that are not correct, then make sure you de-activate these rules. Otherwise you will end up doing clean up over and over again as your discovery process is run.

Best Practice
It is always best to immediately deal with any issues when you see them in an automated system.

In this case if you manually correct the issues, then re-activate the rule. If you cannot immediately take care of the issue, then leave the in a de-activated state and make sure you come up with a remediation plan to get the rule back in place helping you via automation.

5.10 Reconcile Normalization Suggestions

We typically run into these suggestions when have manually normalized and it does not directly match the Central Content Software Library.

In this case, we either need to accept the suggestion provided by the system or reject it. Either way, it is best to take a look and clear the normalization suggestions cue often.

Section 6 – Accountability Phase II – Reconciliation & Remediation

Page Intentionally left blank to preserve
section layout.

www.billcypert.com

6.1 Accountability Phase II – Reconciliation & Remediation Overview

The second part of the Accountability Phase is Reconciliation and Remediation. Although every stage until now has been import, none will yield the immediately actionable results that this stage will. They say you "drive for show and putt for dough", well this is the putting for dough stage. Let's leave the golf analogies here since I am a high handicapper.

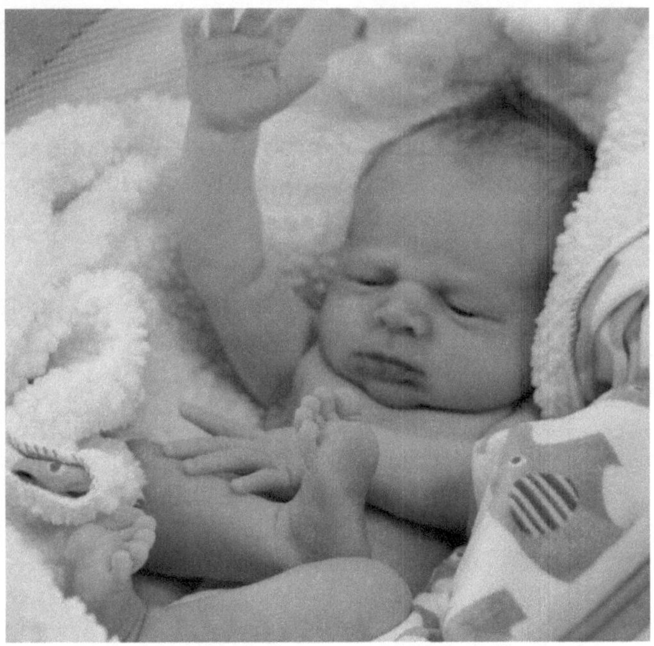

Photo by Orsi Cypert of Kristof Cypert

Best Practice: Start small, care and feed your early wins and watch them grown until you have a solid system that your entire organization will trust.

145

6.2 Scope Software Reconciliation

When we approach reconciliation, it is best to take on bite size efforts rather than trying to "boil the ocean". It is always best to get early easier wins so that everyone from Executive Sponsors to Stakeholders sees the progress and potential of the effort. Therefore, we need to make sure that we have completed the following steps at a minimum:

> **Step 1**. Define the smallest meaningful scope for the reconciliation. My recommendation is that we always start small, get early wins then "rinse and repeat".

> **Step 2.** Ensure all processor definitions are accurate in the Central Software Library and that they have been run.

> **Step 3.** Ensure user and device usage is correct in the Client Access record.

> **Step 4.** Verify groupings are correct. Often if this is based on chargeback (or show back) then this will be based on the appropriate cost center.

6.3 License Position Calculation

Keeping in mind that we are starting with a small sample, it is now time to determine your effective license position. At this point, this is our "educated guess" as to our effective license position.

Once we have our best guess in place, then we will move on to the next step of reviewing the actual results and validating these against what the system is indicating.

Rank and Order is incorporated into the reconciliation engine. This is helpful in eliminating double counts. Ensure that this is working properly by reviewing device and user counts to ensure that we are only reporting one software entitlement rather than two for a user and device.

Additional Considerations

During reconciliation, only 'Licensable' Software Discovery Models are considered.

User allocations are not considered, as they do not apply, when we are reconciling software subscription models.

For an Adobe creative cloud software model, suites will be utilized to reconcile Photoshop, Dreamweaver, etc.

6.4 Software Reconciliation Results

Now we need to review the reconciliation results.

Product Results. Overall compliance position for the given product. Even if there are no software models mapped to the discovery software product, the product result for a discovered licensable product is generated.

Software Model Results. This is compliance of Version and Editions associated with the Product. It is important to understand that Software Entitlements are only reported when there is a corresponding Software Model for the version and edition.

License Metric Results – This displays our current entitlements by user, device and processor. If we have populated the CMDB with has the "Assign To" attribute populated, then we will see information on rights (owned & used), variances on allocations (over & under), allocations (in-use & needed).

> **Note:** If non-compliant result is given then it most often points to the CMDB not having the appropriate attributes populated.

Rights Used by Record. Allocation rights for users and/or devices that are not tied to a subscription model where license count does not apply. If it does not apply, then this field will be blank.

6.5 Remediate Non-Compliant Software

Each non-compliant result should be investigated to determine the best course of action.

Blacklisting Rouge Software. If we do not have an existing Software Model, then we need to create one if the software is valid. Otherwise we should Blacklist the software.

Review the License Metric. When a Software Entitlement exists and we are out of compliance then we must remediate in one of the following ways:

Procure rights required for unlicensed rights.

Remove unlicensed installs.

Allocated not in use. Review each of these careful as this is a great place to save the organization in overallocation situations as well as prevent purchasing un-needed entitlements. In most organizations the standard play is to remove all of these allocations knowing that if a user truly needs the entitlement they can re-request it.

Not allocated in use. Create removal candidates or update the corresponding allocation.

Claim Removal Candidates identified during the Optimize Software Usage process.

6.6 Remediation Actions

Remediation is a key step to keeping your organization compliant. In this step we should do the following:

Allocated not in use. Establish your policies regarding software allocated but not in use. Most organizations leverage a specific time as the guiding policy. As an example, if a user has not used the allocation within the previous 90 days, then they should be alerted to leverage the software or it will be removed after an additional "time out" period.

Not allocated in use. The user should be alerted to request approval for the entitlement. If the approval and subsequent allocation is not performed, then the software will be removed.

Photo by Emile Perron on Unsplash

Section 7 Supporting Materials

Page Intentionally left blank to preserve
section layout.

www.billcypert.com

7.1 Project Success

I often tell customers, other consulting firms and my own teams that in 90+% of projects you can determine if they will succeed or fail by the conclusion of the kick-off meeting. If you have been in consulting for a few years, or decades, like me then you fully understand the cause and effect here.

When the consulting team is very prescriptive with the customer, aligns the outcomes to the appropriate business objectives and seeks to "teach to fish", then they have done their part.

When the customer is clear about what they need, providing the appropriate resources (people, access, governance, etc), and actively participating in the decisions during an implementation, then they have done their part.

Of course, this is only the alignment of the customer organization and the consulting team. The fact is that the vast majority of projects fail to realize their objectives. However, our odds of success are greatly increased if we commit to a comprehensive Organizational Change Management initiative.

7.2 Organizational Change Management

According to McKinsey & Company over 70% of change management programs fail to fulfill their desired objectives. The top reason cited for these failures is employee resistance. If this were only true a small number or organizations or with a small group of people therein, then you could blame the people. However, it is wide spread (>70%) and therefore points to the traditional OCM approach as the primary issue.

Traditional change models view top management as primary creator of change ideas. Team members are relegated to the role of just implementing the change. This removes the input of the very people who would likely have the best input on how to achieve the desired change.

Traditional change model organizations label people sharing concerns and/or providing alternatives as the problem. Therefore, most people "go along to get along" but secretly resent the changes being implemented. Traditional change alienates the very people that it should looking to for insights.

The traditional change model emphasizes that leadership must stay on the path regardless of critical feedback. When critical feedback is withheld or not valued, then projects inevitably fail. Successful projects operate in a true Agile way with built in feed-back loops that not just allow, but rather encourage iteration as we progress towards our project milestones (and outcomes).

The traditional model would lead you to believe that generating team buy in through maximum communication and carrot/stick tactics achieves the best results. However, this is completely the opposite per behavioral research. We must win the hearts and minds of people by valuing their voice in the process. This works perfectly into an Agile iteration approach.

OCM/KPI Dashboard

It's critical that employees have targeted actions to take, but leaders need to assess progress more effectively and to make adjustments as needed. The reason to focus on KPIs during scaling, implementing, and sustaining changes in a digital transformation stems from the need to respond quickly to a rapidly changing environment. Leaders must be able and willing to assess their change programs continually and not be afraid to pivot to higher-value work when the KPIs tell them to do so.

This is why I strongly recommend an OCM dashboard be created for every project. Afterall, how can we all agree with the score unless there is a scoreboard?

OCM High Level Approach

Developing acceptance and support, is a necessary component for successfully managing change within a business. It doesn't matter whether this is a big change or a little one, or whether it is driven by internal processes or the external market. People will need to change for the project to be a success.

People may have to alter their behavior, adopt new mindsets, learn and adapt to new processes and practices, adhere to a different set of policies, or make any number of other changes. All the people involved with the proposed change, aka "the stakeholders," must be on board and committed for this project to be a success.

1. Plan, plan and plan. Carefully.

This is truly the embodiment of the Covey "begin with the end in mind" mantra. In order to implement successful changes, you will need to imagine what the best possible end result will look like once it's all said and done. With this vision in place, then it's a matter of listing and documenting the necessary tasks to accomplish it, and outlining how, and by whom, these tasks will be completed.

2. Define Governance.

Every successful change management project has a well-defined governance, which is basically the framework for making decisions and the set of pre-determined processes for implementing those decisions. Structures, roles and responsibilities must be established throughout each level of the organization in order to support change and keep stakeholders engaged.

3. Assignment of Resources.

It's important that you establish dedicated organizational leaders, both at the top and throughout the organization, to keep the change management process stable. The criteria here is not title, but rather who can get the things done that need to be done.

4. Expect & Welcome Iterations

The end goal is all that matters. Therefore, break each outcome into the most atomic level and go for that success. As you do each thing that can be tested on end users, do it and incorporate their feedback into your next iteration. There are few things more disappointing than working on something for months only to find out end users don't or can't use it.

5. Find Early Adopters and Key Influencers

There should be at least a few people who are ready to adopt the change early on, and these stakeholders can become your biggest advocates to help get other folks on board with the transition. Good advocates, of course, should also demonstrate strong leadership abilities as well as other professional and personal strengths that attract respect from others. By identifying these advocates early on, and providing them with additional training and engagement, you can set a more positive tone that will ensure a smoother process with fewer hiccups.

6. Constantly Assess and Review.

The scoreboard is all that matters. Therefore, have everyone looking at the same scoreboard throughout the project. In our case, we always built an OCM/KPI Dashboard so that everyone is aligned on the project status.

In Conclusion

We need to approach Organizational Change Management in a new way that reflects an iterative application of the Crossing the Chasm model. My strong advocation is that we need to win hearts and minds to succeed in the OCM rather than the traditional model which to me feels closer to a dictatorship style. My grandfather used to always say "one convinced against their will is of the same opinion still". The wisdom he recited seems very appropriate when we think about how to succeed in Organization Change.

7.3 Setting up SAM on SN

How to Request Software Asset Management

ServiceNow must activate the SAM plugin as it requires an additional subscription. You may request the plugin for free in a sub-production instance, otherwise you will need the appropriate SN license.

> Request the SAM plugin (**com.snc.samp**) via a HI Service Portal request.

Additional helpful plugins can be requested on an individual basis in the same way.

> Request (**com.sn_samp_master**) to load all of the publisher packs in addition to the SAM Pro plugin.

> Request (**com.sn.samp_usage_sccm**) for Integration with MS SCCM 2k12 v2

> Request (**com.sn.samp_usage_sccm_2016**) for Integration with MS SCCM 2k16

> Request Orchestration to automate software installs and uninstalls on devices (**com.snc.orchestration.client_sf_distribu tion**)

Roles added with SAM

sam_user. Has permission to access all non-administrative SAM features.

sam_admin. Has permission to manage reclamation and initiate reconciliation in addition to inheriting all sam_user permissions.

sam_developer. Has permission to write scripts as well as perform all sam_admin tasks.

7.4 SAM Dashboards Explained

One of the best features of ServiceNow is the visibility that it brings to your organization. The dashboards that are provided OOB (out-of-box) from SN SAM are outstanding. Over the next few pages, I will walk you through the metrics that are displayed on the following dashboards:

Software Asset Analytics – Overview
Software Asset Analytics – License Summary
Software Asset Analytics – Compliance Summary
Software Asset Analytics – Removal Summary

Normalization and Content Service

Software Publisher Analytics - Microsoft
Software Publisher Analytics - Oracle
Software Publisher Analytics - IBM
Software Publisher Analytics - VMware
Software Publisher Analytics - Citrix
Software Publisher Analytics - SAP

Software Asset Analytics Dashboard

This dashboard shows compliance, removal summaries, true-up costs and licenses.

Overview Tab

Total True-Up Cost. Cost to be compliant based on the
average prices in entitlements for the rights.

Publishers out of Compliance. Number of publishers that have at least one software model out of compliance.

Products out of Compliance. Number of products that have at least one software model out of compliance.

Potential Savings. Cost saved if removal candidates are reclaimed.

True-up Cost Breakdown. Cost to be compliant based on the average prices in entitlements for the rights by publisher.

Software Spend Breakdown. Total software cost of all
entitlements not retired by publisher.

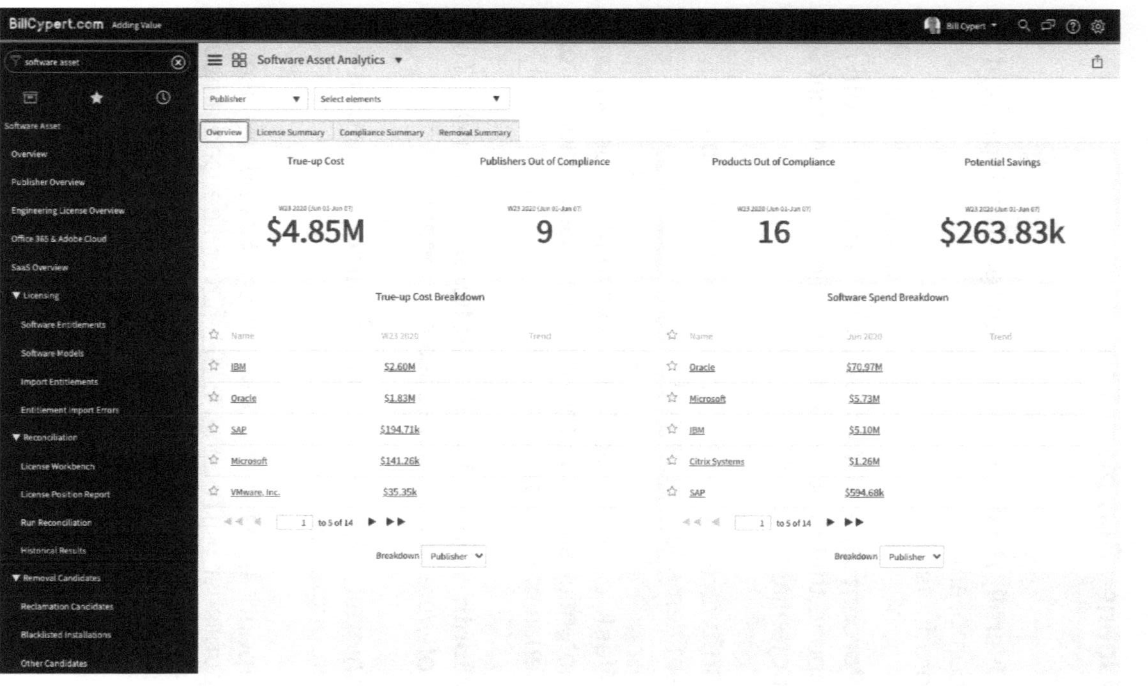

BillCypert.com Adding Value
Bill Cypert
software asset
Software Asset Analytics
Publisher
Select elements
Overview License Summary Compliance Summary Removal Summary
Software Asset
Overview
Publisher Overview
Engineering License Overview
Office 365 & Adobe Cloud
SaaS Overview
Licensing
Software Entitlements
Software Models
Import Entitlements
Entitlement Import Errors
Reconciliation
License Workbench
License Position Report
Run Reconciliation
Historical Results
Removal Candidates
Reclamation Candidates
Blacklisted Installations
Other Candidates
True-up Cost
Publishers Out of Compliance
Products Out of Compliance
Potential Savings
W23 2020 (Jun 01-Jun 07)
$4.85M
9
16
$263.83k
True-up Cost Breakdown
Software Spend Breakdown
Name W23 2020 Trend
IBM $2.60M
Oracle $1.83M
SAP $194.71k
Microsoft $141.26k
VMware, Inc. $35.35k
1 to 5 of 14
Breakdown Publisher
Name Jun 2020 Trend
Oracle $70.97M
Microsoft $5.73M
IBM $5.10M
Citrix Systems $1.26M
SAP $594.68k
1 to 5 of 14
Breakdown Publisher

License Summary Tab

Overall Product Compliance. Total percent of compliant
products.

Percent Spend Not in Use. Percent of software spend that is not in use (over-licensed amount and potential savings).

Software Spend. Total software cost of all entitlements not retired.

Week over Week Cost Summary. True-up cost, potential savings, and over-licensed amount for a series of weeks.

Month Over Month Software Spend. Total software spend in a series of months.

Overall Publisher Compliance. Percent of products compliant by publisher.

Spend In Use by Publisher. Spend in use by publisher = [[Total spend] - [Over-licensed amount] - [Potential savings]] / Total spend.

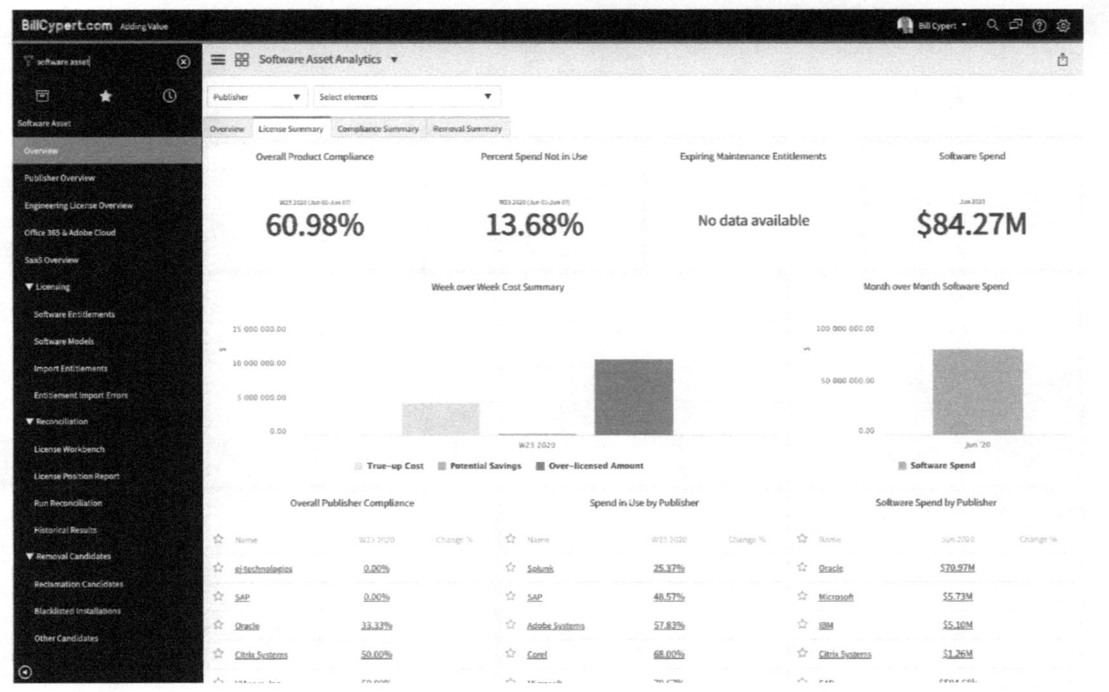

BillCypert.com Adding Value
Bill Cypert
software asset
Software Asset
Software Asset Analytics
Publisher
Select elements
Overview
License Summary
Compliance Summary
Removal Summary
Overview
Publisher Overview
Engineering License Overview
Office 365 & Adobe Cloud
SaaS Overview
Licensing
Software Entitlements
Software Models
Import Entitlements
Entitlement Import Errors
Reconciliation
License Workbench
License Position Report
Run Reconciliation
Historical Results
Removal Candidates
Reclamation Candidates
Blacklisted Installations
Other Candidates
Overall Product Compliance
Percent Spend Not in Use
Expiring Maintenance Entitlements
Software Spend
W23 2020 (Jun 01-Jun 07)
60.98%
W23 2020 (Jun 01-Jun 07)
13.68%
No data available
Jun 2020
$84.27M
Week over Week Cost Summary
Month over Month Software Spend
15 000 000.00
10 000 000.00
5 000 000.00
0.00
W23 2020
True-up Cost   Potential Savings   Over-licensed Amount
100 000 000.00
50 000 000.00
0.00
Jun '20
Software Spend
Overall Publisher Compliance
Name   W23 2020   Change %
ej-technologies   0.00%
SAP   0.00%
Oracle   33.33%
Citrix Systems   50.00%
Spend in Use by Publisher
Name   W23 2020   Change %
Splunk   25.37%
SAP   48.57%
Adobe Systems   57.83%
Corel   68.00%
Software Spend by Publisher
Name   Jun 2020   Change %
Oracle $70.97M
Microsoft $5.73M
IBM $5.10M
Citrix Systems $1.26M

True-up Cost. Cost to be compliant based on the average prices for entitlements for the rights.

Publishers out of compliance. Number of publishers that have at least one software model out of compliance.

Products out of compliance. Number of products that have at least one software model out of compliance.

Potential savings. Cost saved if removal candidates are reclaimed.

Breakdowns. Shows the detailed list of results based on the widget selected. Breakdowns include Publisher, Product, and Scorecard.

Records. Shows the detailed list of product results based on the widget selected.

Over-licensed amount. Cost of licenses owned but not being used.

Publishers over-licensed. Number of publishers that have at least one software right not being used.

Products over-licensed. Number of products that have at least one software right not being used.

Breakdowns. Shows the detailed list of results based on the widget selected. Breakdowns include Publisher, Product, and Scorecard.

Records. Shows the detailed list of product results based on the widget selected.

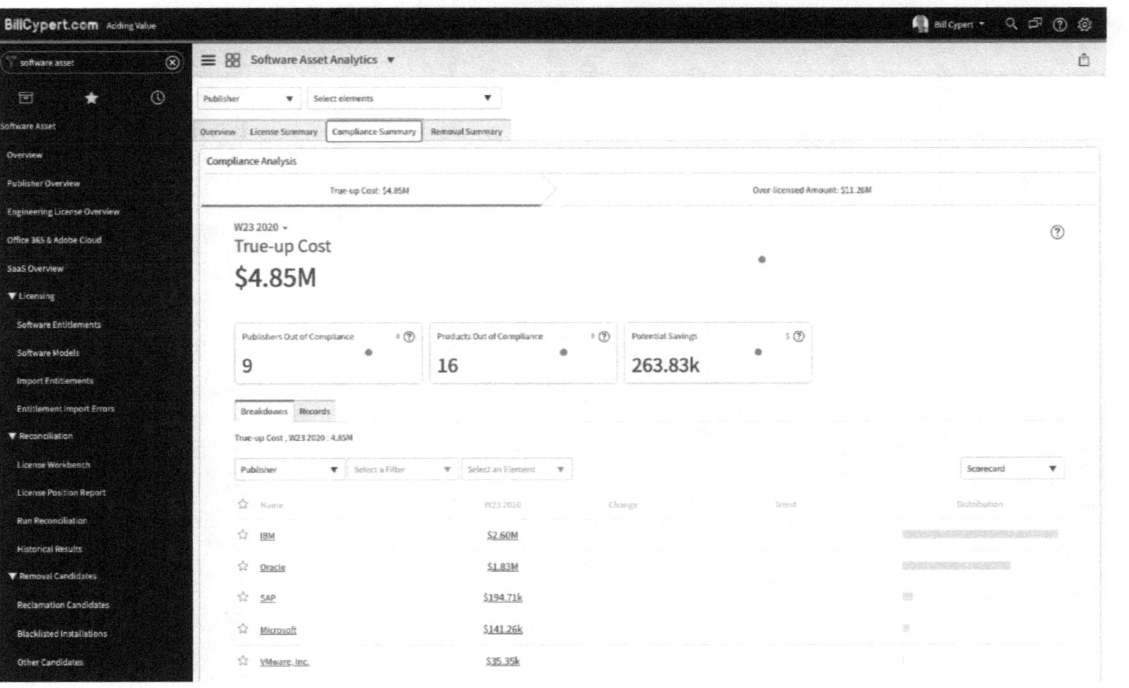

BillCypert.com Adding Value
Bill Cypert
software asset
Software Asset
Overview
Publisher Overview
Engineering License Overview
Office 365 & Adobe Cloud
SaaS Overview
Licensing
Software Entitlements
Software Models
Import Entitlements
Entitlement Import Errors
Reconciliation
License Workbench
License Position Report
Run Reconciliation
Historical Results
Removal Candidates
Reclamation Candidates
Blacklisted Installations
Other Candidates
Software Asset Analytics
Publisher
Select elements
Overview   License Summary   Compliance Summary   Removal Summary
Compliance Analysis
True-up Cost: $4.85M
Over-licensed Amount: $11.26M
W23 2020
True-up Cost
$4.85M
Publishers Out of Compliance
9
Products Out of Compliance
16
Potential Savings
263.83k
Breakdowns   Records
True-up Cost , W23 2020 : 4.85M
Publisher   Select a Filter   Select an Element
Scorecard
Name   W23 2020   Change   Trend   Distribution
IBM $2.60M
Oracle $1.83M
SAP $194.71k
Microsoft $141.26k
VMware, Inc. $35.35k

True-up Cost. Cost to be compliant based on the average prices for entitlements for the rights.

Publishers out of compliance. Number of publishers that have at least one software model out of compliance.

Products out of compliance. Number of products that have at least one software model out of compliance.

Potential savings. Cost saved if removal candidates are reclaimed.

Breakdowns. Shows the detailed list of results based on the widget selected. Breakdowns include Publisher, Product, and Scorecard.

Records. Shows the detailed list of product results based on the widget selected.

Over-licensed amount. Cost of licenses owned but not being used.

Publishers over-licensed. Number of publishers that have at least one software right not being used.

Products over-licensed. Number of products that have at least one software right not being used.

Breakdowns. Shows the detailed list of results based on the widget selected. Breakdowns include Publisher, Product, and Scorecard.

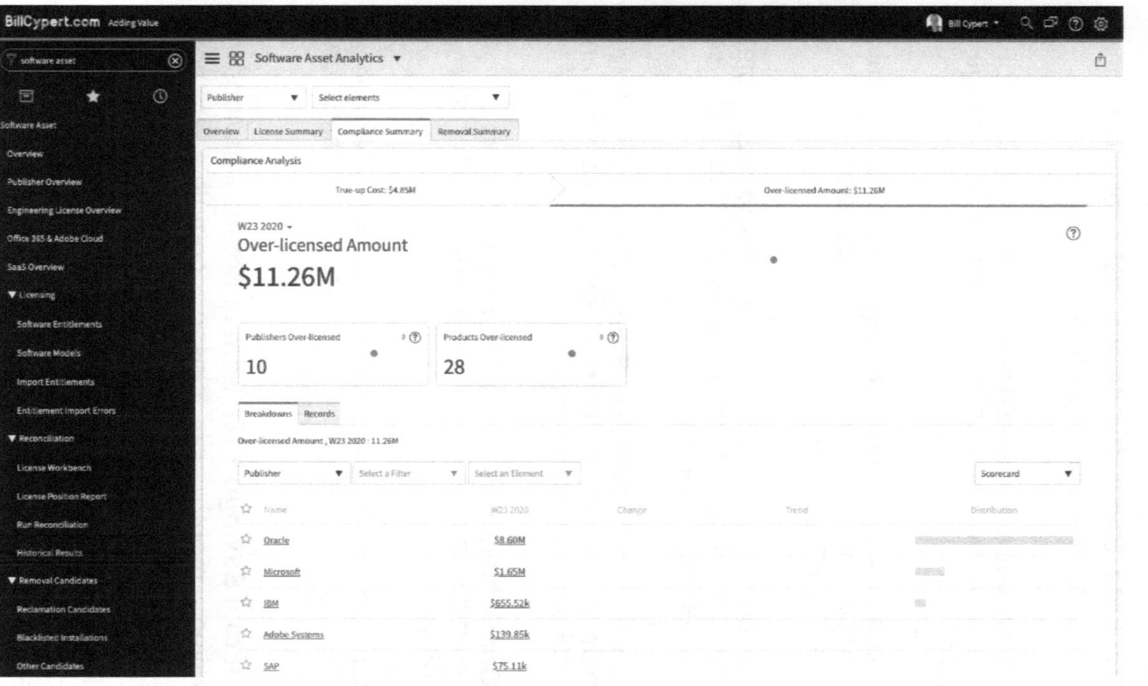

BillCypert.com Adding Value
Bill Cypert
Software Asset Analytics
software asset
Software Asset
Overview
Publisher Overview
Engineering License Overview
Office 365 & Adobe Cloud
SaaS Overview
Licensing
Software Entitlements
Software Models
Import Entitlements
Entitlement Import Errors
Reconciliation
License Workbench
License Position Report
Run Reconciliation
Historical Results
Removal Candidates
Reclamation Candidates
Blacklisted Installations
Other Candidates
Publisher
Select elements
Overview   License Summary   Compliance Summary   Removal Summary
Compliance Analysis
True-up Cost: $4.85M
Over-licensed Amount: $11.26M
W23 2020
Over-licensed Amount
$11.26M
Publishers Over-licensed
10
Products Over-licensed
28
Breakdowns   Records
Over-licensed Amount , W23 2020 : 11.26M
Publisher
Select a Filter
Select an Element
Scorecard
Name   W23 2020   Change   Trend   Distribution
Oracle $8.60M
Microsoft $1.65M
IBM $655.52k
Adobe Systems $139.85k
SAP $75.11k

Records. Shows the detailed list of product results based on the widget selected.

Reclamation Candidates. Total number of active removal candidates with a low usage justification.

Blacklisted Installs Being Removed. Total number of active removal candidates with a blacklisted justification.

Unlicensed Installs Being Removed. Total number of active removal candidates with an unlicensed justification.

Unallocated Installs Being Removed. Total number of active removal candidates with an unallocated justification.

Candidates Requiring Attention. Number of removal candidates in the attention required state.

Candidates Not Updated in 30 Days. Number of removal candidates that have an updated date value older than 30 days.

Actual Savings YTD. Sum of potential savings in a given month of closed complete removal candidates.

Removal Candidates Breakdown. Active removal candidates in various breakdowns (State, Publisher, Product, Justification, and Last Updated).

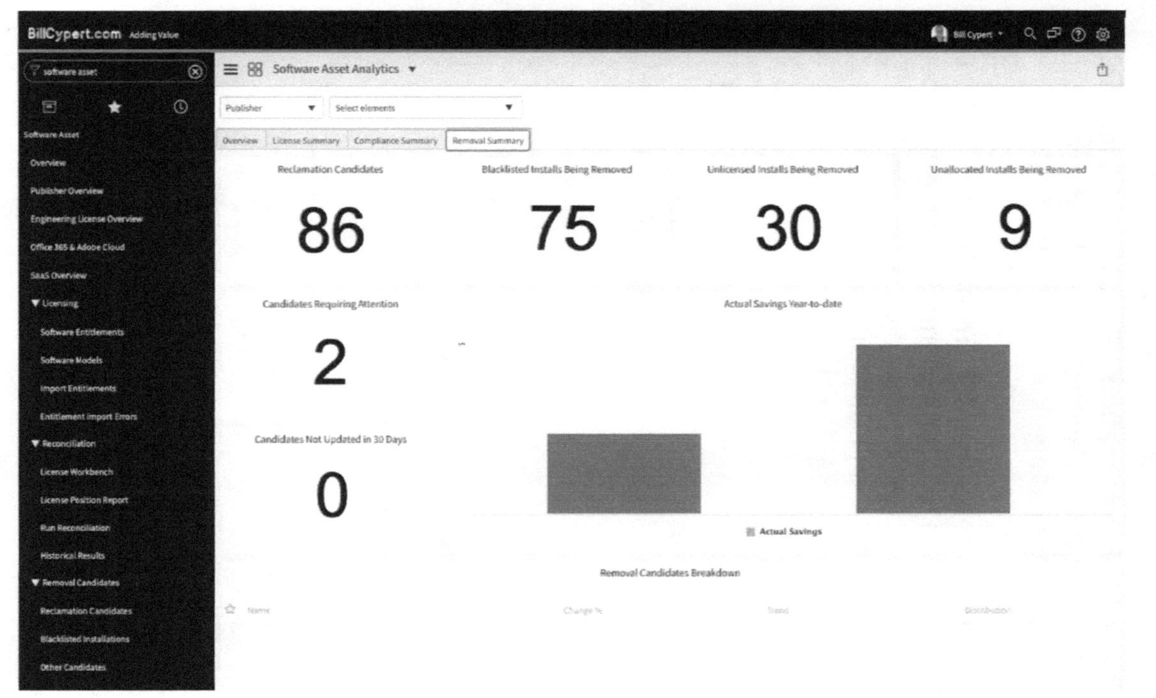

BillCypert.com Adding Value
Bill Cypert
software asset
Software Asset Analytics
Publisher
Select elements
Overview | License Summary | Compliance Summary | Removal Summary
Reclamation Candidates
86
Blacklisted Installs Being Removed
75
Unlicensed Installs Being Removed
30
Unallocated Installs Being Removed
9
Candidates Requiring Attention
2
Actual Savings Year-to-date
Candidates Not Updated in 30 Days
0
Actual Savings
Removal Candidates Breakdown
Name
Change %
Trend
Distribution
Software Asset
Overview
Publisher Overview
Engineering License Overview
Office 365 & Adobe Cloud
SaaS Overview
Licensing
Software Entitlements
Software Models
Import Entitlements
Entitlement Import Errors
Reconciliation
License Workbench
License Position Report
Run Reconciliation
Historical Results
Removal Candidates
Reclamation Candidates
Blacklisted Installations
Other Candidates

Overall Normalization Rates for Licensable Software. Overall normalization status count for all licensable products.

Normalization Rate Breakdown for Top Publishers. Licensable normalization status count per top publisher for Microsoft, Oracle, IBM, VMware, Citrix, and Adobe.

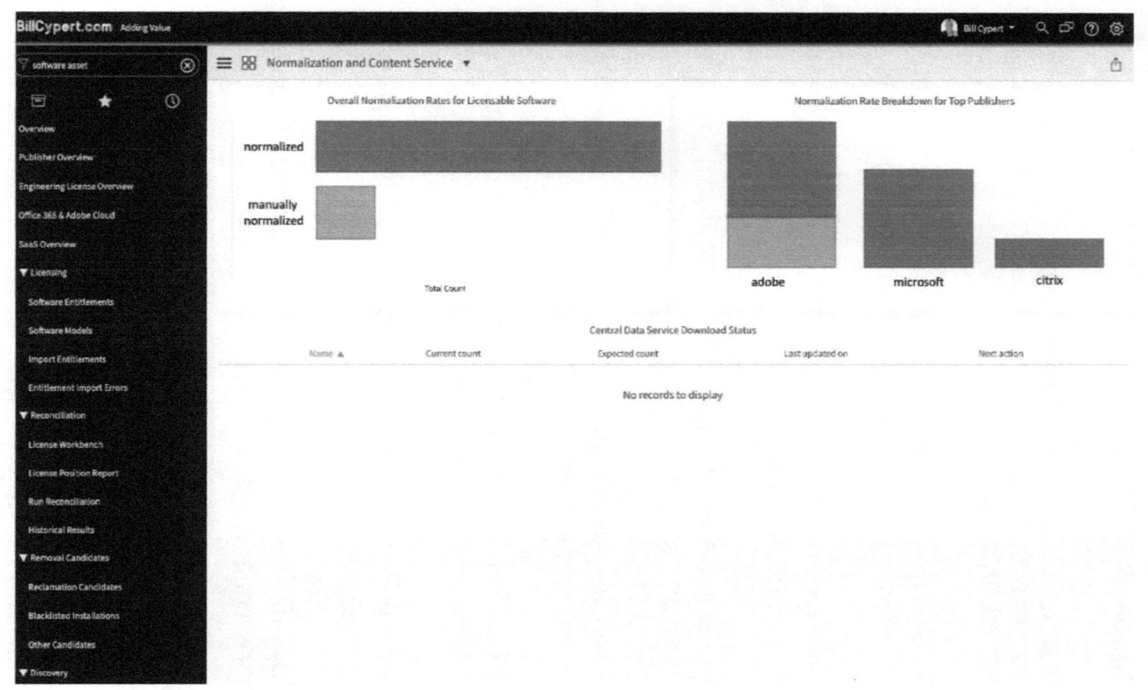

BillCypert.com Adding Value
Bill Cypert
software asset
Normalization and Content Service
Overview
Publisher Overview
Engineering License Overview
Office 365 & Adobe Cloud
SaaS Overview
Licensing
Software Entitlements
Software Models
Import Entitlements
Entitlement Import Errors
Reconciliation
License Workbench
License Position Report
Run Reconciliation
Historical Results
Removal Candidates
Reclamation Candidates
Blacklisted Installations
Other Candidates
Discovery
Overall Normalization Rates for Licensable Software
normalized
manually normalized
Total Count
Normalization Rate Breakdown for Top Publishers
adobe
microsoft
citrix
Central Data Service Download Status
Name
Current count
Expected count
Last updated on
Next action
No records to display

Microsoft

Products out of Compliance. Number of products that have at least one software model out of compliance.

Total True-up Cost. Cost to be compliant based on the average prices for entitlements for the rights.

Over-Licensed Amount. Cost of licenses owned but not being used.

Reclamations Requiring Attention. State is Attention Required.

Potential Savings. Cost saved if removal candidates are reclaimed.

Actual Savings Year-to-date. Closed on This Year AND State is Closed Complete.

Top 10 Products by True-up Cost. Greatest true-up costs by product.

Top 10 Products by Potential Savings. Greatest potential savings by product.

Top Product Risk Based on Lifecycle Phase. Heat map of software model lifecycles, including those about to change to the next phase. The highest value is red and the lowest value is white.

SQL Server Install Breakdown. Total software installations per SQL Server.

SQL Server Active Right Breakdown. Number of total active rights per SQL Server.

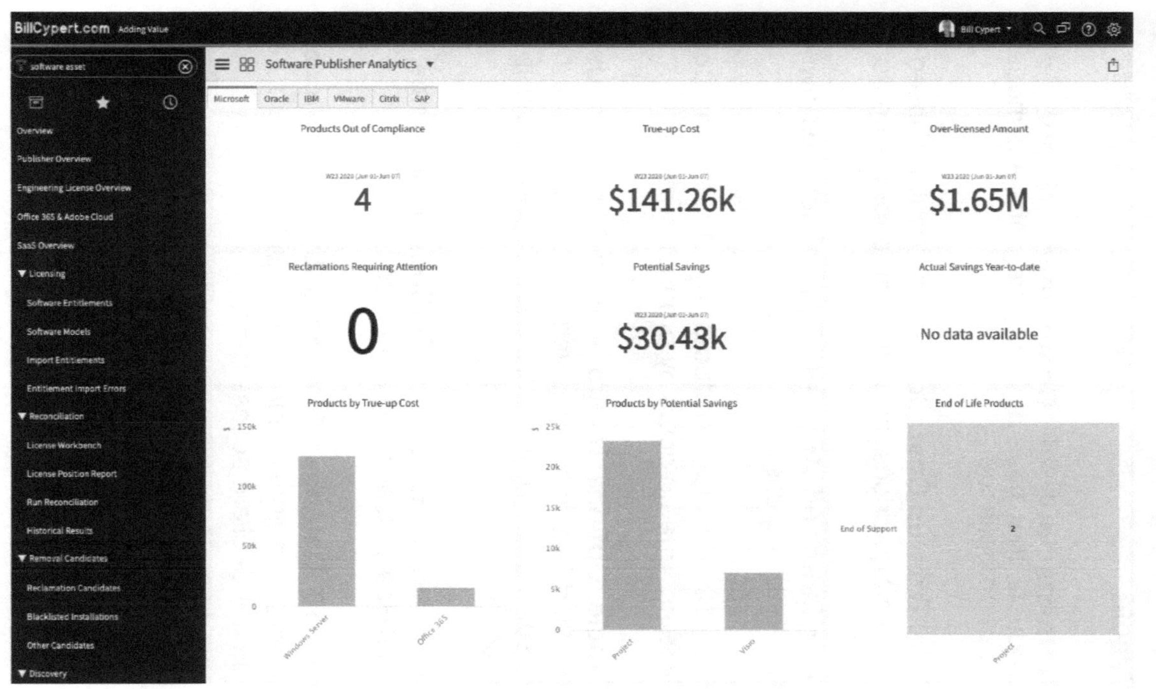

BillCypert.com Adding Value
Bill Cypert
software asset
Overview
Publisher Overview
Engineering License Overview
Office 365 & Adobe Cloud
SaaS Overview
Licensing
Software Entitlements
Software Models
Import Entitlements
Entitlement Import Errors
Reconciliation
License Workbench
License Position Report
Run Reconciliation
Historical Results
Removal Candidates
Reclamation Candidates
Blacklisted Installations
Other Candidates
Discovery
Software Publisher Analytics
Microsoft Oracle IBM VMware Citrix SAP
Products Out of Compliance
W23 2020 (Jun 01-Jun 07)
4
True-up Cost
W23 2020 (Jun 01-Jun 07)
$141.26k
Over-licensed Amount
W23 2020 (Jun 01-Jun 07)
$1.65M
Reclamations Requiring Attention
0
Potential Savings
W23 2020 (Jun 01-Jun 07)
$30.43k
Actual Savings Year-to-date
No data available
Products by True-up Cost
150k
100k
50k
0
Windows Server
Office 365
Products by Potential Savings
25k
20k
15k
10k
5k
0
Project
Visio
End of Life Products
End of Support
2
Project

Oracle

Products out of Compliance. Number of products that have at least one software model out of compliance.

Total True-up Cost. Cost to be compliant based on the average prices for entitlements for the rights.

Over-Licensed Amount. Cost of licenses owned but not being used.

Top 10 Oracle Products by True- up Cost. Greatest true-up costs by product.

Oracle Options Usage - (Installed vs In Use). Installed Oracle licenses versus licenses in use (true versus false). Time frame used to determine if an option is in use is 365 days.

Database Instances by Edition. Total number of database instances by database edition.

Top 10 Database Instances by Client Access Users. Database instances with the greatest number of client access users.

Top Product Risk Based on Lifecycle Phase. Heat map of software model lifecycles, including those about to change to the next phase. The highest value is red and the lowest value is white.

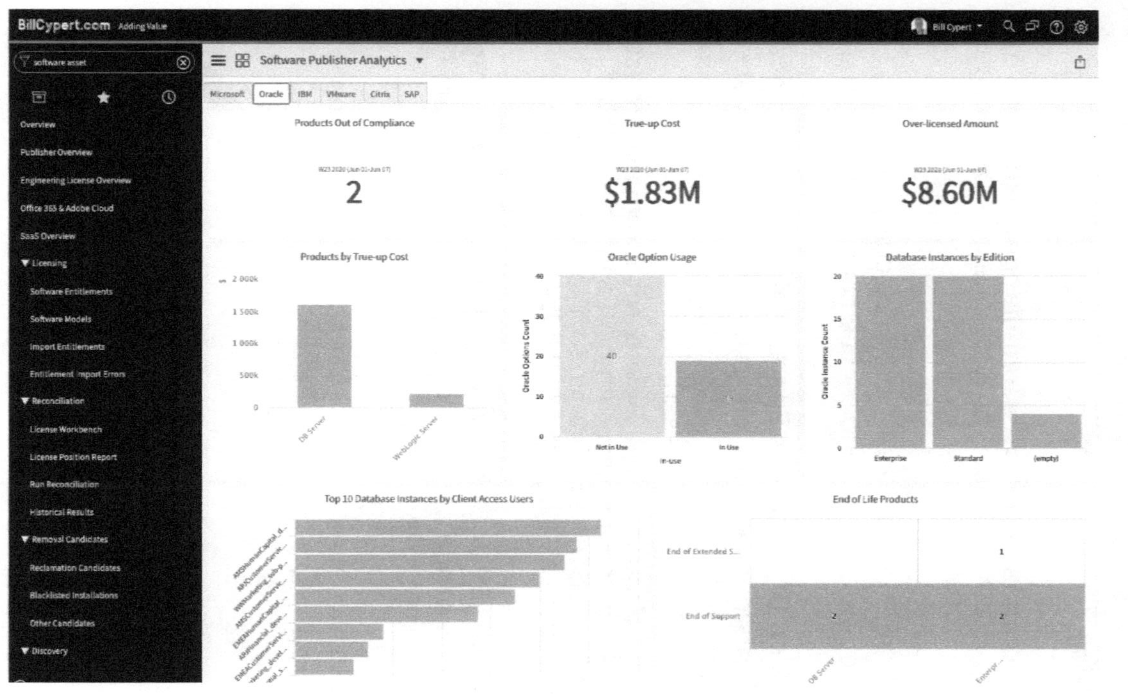
BillCypert.com Adding Value
Bill Cypert
software asset
Software Publisher Analytics
Microsoft Oracle IBM VMware Citrix SAP
Overview
Publisher Overview
Engineering License Overview
Office 365 & Adobe Cloud
SaaS Overview
Licensing
Software Entitlements
Software Models
Import Entitlements
Entitlement Import Errors
Reconciliation
License Workbench
License Position Report
Run Reconciliation
Historical Results
Removal Candidates
Reclamation Candidates
Blacklisted Installations
Other Candidates
Discovery
Products Out of Compliance
W23 2020 (Jun 01-Jun 07)
2
True-up Cost
W23 2020 (Jun 01-Jun 07)
$1.83M
Over-licensed Amount
W23 2020 (Jun 01-Jun 07)
$8.60M
Products by True-up Cost
2 000k
1 500k
1 000k
500k
0
DB Server
WebLogic Server
Oracle Option Usage
Oracle Options Count
40
30
20
10
0
Not in Use
In Use
In-use
Database Instances by Edition
Oracle Instance Count
20
15
10
5
0
Enterprise
Standard
(empty)
Top 10 Database Instances by Client Access Users
End of Life Products
End of Extended S...
1
End of Support
2
2
DB Server
Enterpr...

IBM

Products out of Compliance. Number of products that have at least one software model out of compliance.

Total True-up Cost. Cost to be compliant based on the average prices for entitlements for the rights.

% of Total Excess Spend Not In Use. Sum of the over-licensed amount over the total of licensed amount.

Top Product Risk Based on Lifecycle Phase. Heat map of software model lifecycles, including those about to change to the next phase. The highest value is red and the lowest value is white.

Total PVU Sub-capacity Consumption Trend. Comparison of the aggregate peak consumption for all products over time.

PVU Sub-capacity Breakdown of Top 10 Products. Peak PVU utilization for the top 10 IBM products.

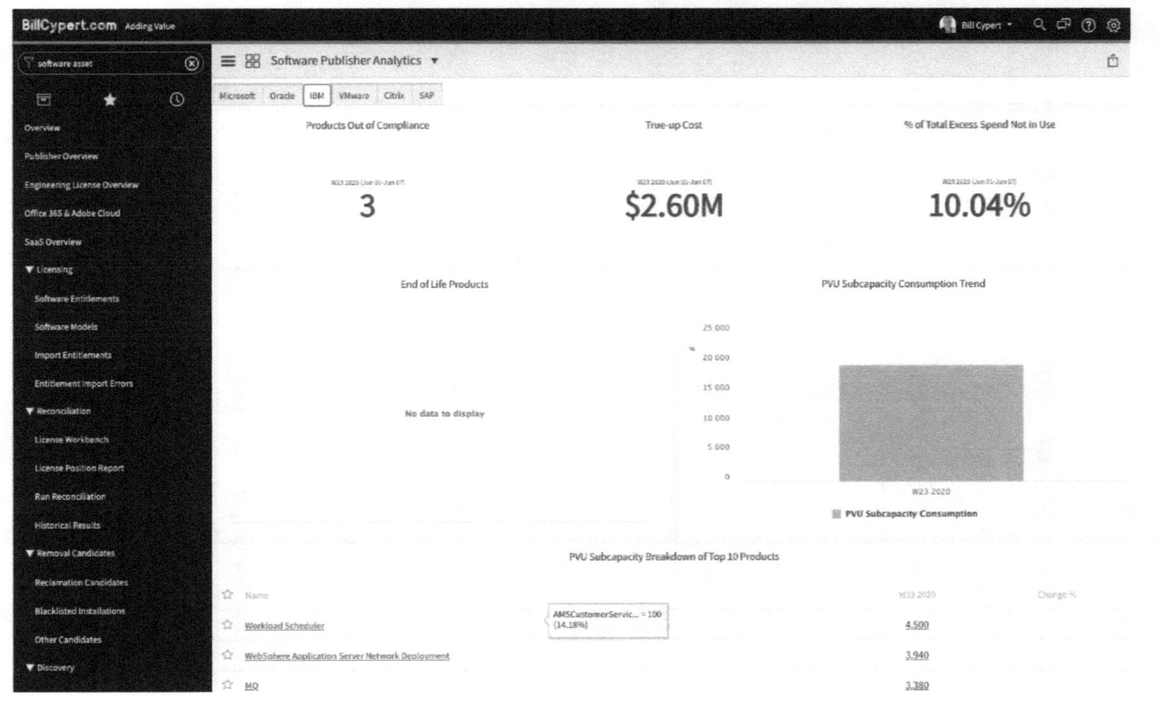
BillCypert.com Adding Value
Bill Cypert
software asset
Software Publisher Analytics
Microsoft   Oracle   IBM   VMware   Citrix   SAP
Overview
Publisher Overview
Engineering License Overview
Office 365 & Adobe Cloud
SaaS Overview
Licensing
Software Entitlements
Software Models
Import Entitlements
Entitlement Import Errors
Reconciliation
License Workbench
License Position Report
Run Reconciliation
Historical Results
Removal Candidates
Reclamation Candidates
Blacklisted Installations
Other Candidates
Discovery
Products Out of Compliance
W23 2020 (Jun 01-Jun 07)
3
True-up Cost
W23 2020 (Jun 01-Jun 07)
$2.60M
% of Total Excess Spend Not in Use
W23 2020 (Jun 01-Jun 07)
10.04%
End of Life Products
No data to display
PVU Subcapacity Consumption Trend
25 000
20 000
15 000
10 000
5 000
0
W23 2020
PVU Subcapacity Consumption
PVU Subcapacity Breakdown of Top 10 Products
Name
AMSCustomerServic... = 100
(14.18%)
W23 2020
Change %
Workload Scheduler
4,500
WebSphere Application Server Network Deployment
3,940
MQ
3,380

VMware

Products out of Compliance. Number of products that have at least one software model out of compliance.

Over-licensed Amount. Cost of licenses owned but not being used.

True-up Cost. Cost to be compliant based on the average prices for entitlements for the rights.

Top 5 Installed Products. Count of top 5 VMware products installed.

vSphere Territorial Non-compliance. Compliance of vCenter deployments. Drill down on the location to filter.

ESX Servers by Region. Location, ESX count, CPU count, and cores count.

Audit View. VSphere deployments: Product, License Key, Used By, Assigned To, Location, CPU core count, CPU count, vCenter reference, evaluation expiration date, and software install.

Top Product Risk Based on Lifecycle Phase. Heat map of software model lifecycles, including those about to change to the next phase. The highest value is red and the lowest value is white.

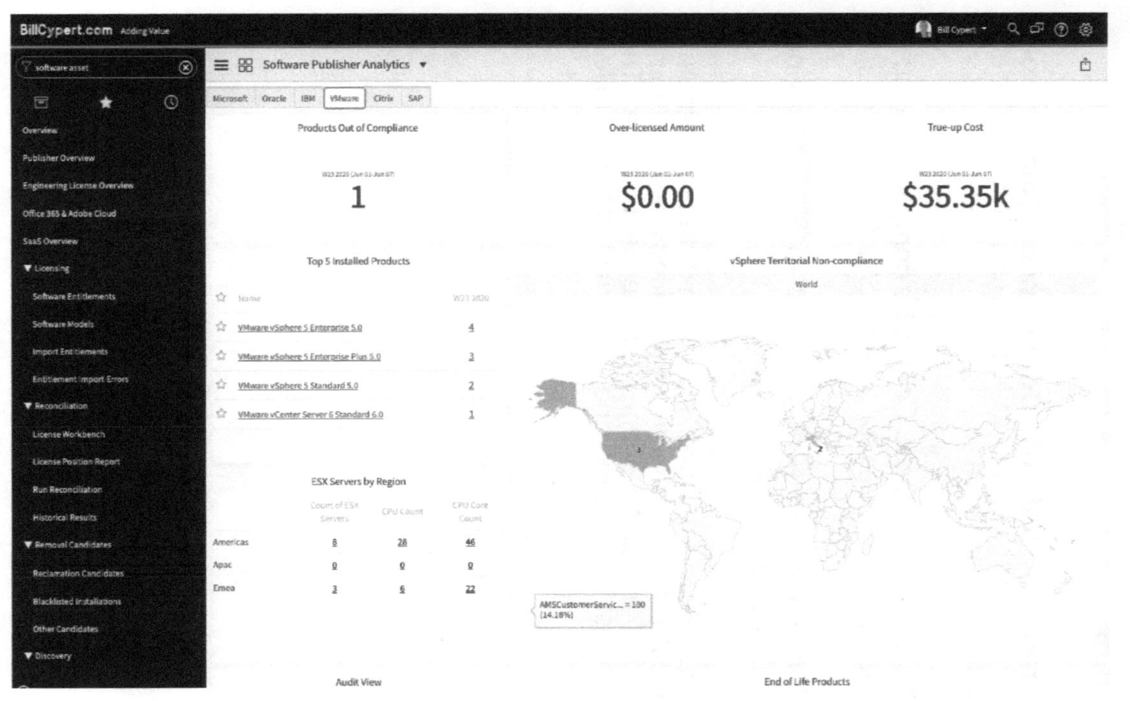

BillCypert.com Adding Value
Bill Cypert
software asset
Software Publisher Analytics
Microsoft   Oracle   IBM   VMware   Citrix   SAP
Overview
Publisher Overview
Engineering License Overview
Office 365 & Adobe Cloud
SaaS Overview
Licensing
Software Entitlements
Software Models
Import Entitlements
Entitlement Import Errors
Reconciliation
License Workbench
License Position Report
Run Reconciliation
Historical Results
Removal Candidates
Reclamation Candidates
Blacklisted Installations
Other Candidates
Discovery
Products Out of Compliance
W23 2020 (Jun 01-Jun 07)
1
Over-licensed Amount
W23 2020 (Jun 01-Jun 07)
$0.00
True-up Cost
W23 2020 (Jun 01-Jun 07)
$35.35k
Top 5 Installed Products
Name
W23 2020
VMware vSphere 5 Enterprise 5.0
4
VMware vSphere 5 Enterprise Plus 5.0
3
VMware vSphere 5 Standard 5.0
2
VMware vCenter Server 6 Standard 6.0
1
ESX Servers by Region
Count of ESX Servers   CPU Count   CPU Core Count
Americas   8   28   46
Apac   0   0   0
Emea   3   6   22
vSphere Territorial Non-compliance
World
AMSCustomerServic... = 100 (14.18%)
Audit View
End of Life Products

Citrix

Products out of Compliance. Number of products that have at least one software model out of compliance.

Total True-up Cost. Cost to be compliant based on the average prices for entitlements for the rights.

Over-Licensed Amount. Cost of licenses owned but not being used.

Top Product Risk Based on Lifecycle Phase. Heat map of software model lifecycles, including those about to change to the next phase. The highest value is red and the lowest value is white.

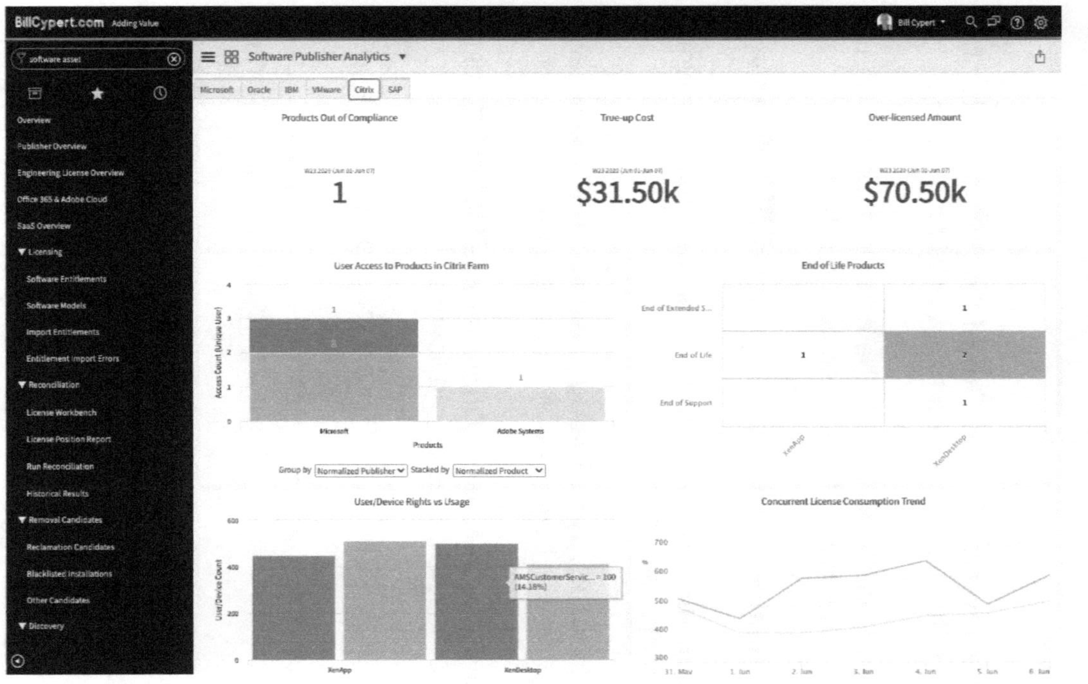

BillCypert.com Adding Value
Bill Cypert
software asset
Software Publisher Analytics
Microsoft Oracle IBM VMware Citrix SAP
Overview
Publisher Overview
Engineering License Overview
Office 365 & Adobe Cloud
SaaS Overview
Licensing
Software Entitlements
Software Models
Import Entitlements
Entitlement Import Errors
Reconciliation
License Workbench
License Position Report
Run Reconciliation
Historical Results
Removal Candidates
Reclamation Candidates
Blacklisted Installations
Other Candidates
Discovery
Products Out of Compliance
True-up Cost
Over-licensed Amount
1
$31.50k
$70.50k
User Access to Products in Citrix Farm
End of Life Products
Access Count (Unique User)
Microsoft
Adobe Systems
Products
End of Extended S...
End of Life
End of Support
XenApp
XenDesktop
Group by Normalized Publisher Stacked by Normalized Product
User/Device Rights vs Usage
Concurrent License Consumption Trend
User/Device Count
XenApp
XenDesktop
AMSCustomerServic... = 100 (14.18%)
31. May 1. Jun 2. Jun 3. Jun 4. Jun 5. Jun 6. Jun

SAP

Named User Types Out of Compliance. Number of software models that are out of compliance.

True-up Cost. Cost to be compliant based on the average prices for entitlements for the rights.

Potential Savings. Cost saved removal candidates.

Over-licensed Amount. Cost of licenses owned but not being used.

Licensed Non-Dialog Users. SAP non-dialog users that have a named user assignment.

SAP Locked Users Consuming a License. Locked SAP users consuming a license.

Inactive Users. SAP users logged +90 days ago.

System Users Without a Named User Assignment. SAP users who do not have a named user assignment.

Total Named User Count Distribution. Number of total licenses distributed for named users.

Named User Types True-up Cost Breakdown. Software models w/named users & cost to true them up.

Unique User Growth Year-To- Date. Number of unique users that are in the SAP system monthly.

Client Distribution. Number of SAP clients and their licenses.

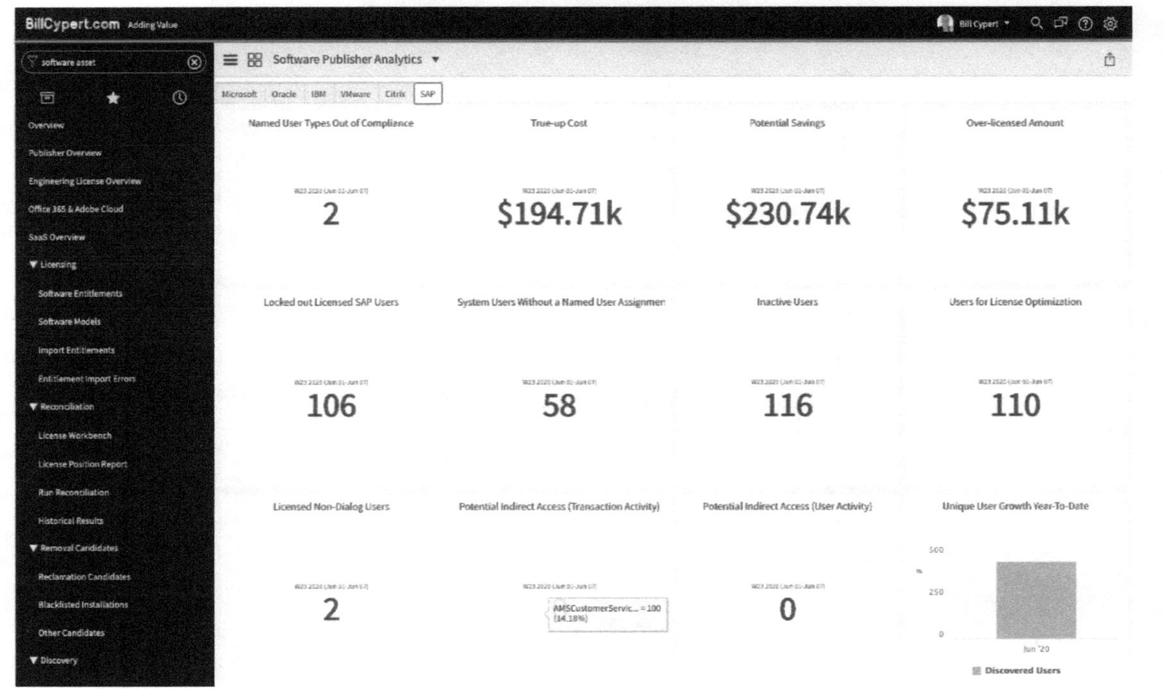

BillCypert.com Adding Value
Bill Cypert
software asset
Overview
Publisher Overview
Engineering License Overview
Office 365 & Adobe Cloud
SaaS Overview
Licensing
Software Entitlements
Software Models
Import Entitlements
Entitlement Import Errors
Reconciliation
License Workbench
License Position Report
Run Reconciliation
Historical Results
Removal Candidates
Reclamation Candidates
Blacklisted Installations
Other Candidates
Discovery
Software Publisher Analytics
Microsoft   Oracle   IBM   VMware   Citrix   SAP
Named User Types Out of Compliance
W23 2020 (Jun 01-Jun 07)
2
True-up Cost
W23 2020 (Jun 01-Jun 07)
$194.71k
Potential Savings
W23 2020 (Jun 01-Jun 07)
$230.74k
Over-licensed Amount
W23 2020 (Jun 01-Jun 07)
$75.11k
Locked out Licensed SAP Users
W23 2020 (Jun 01-Jun 07)
106
System Users Without a Named User Assignment
W23 2020 (Jun 01-Jun 07)
58
Inactive Users
W23 2020 (Jun 01-Jun 07)
116
Users for License Optimization
W23 2020 (Jun 01-Jun 07)
110
Licensed Non-Dialog Users
W23 2020 (Jun 01-Jun 07)
2
Potential Indirect Access (Transaction Activity)
W23 2020 (Jun 01-Jun 07)
AMSCustomerServic... = 100
(14.18%)
Potential Indirect Access (User Activity)
W23 2020 (Jun 01-Jun 07)
0
Unique User Growth Year-To-Date
500
250
0
Jun '20
Discovered Users

Page Intentionally left blank to preserve
section layout.

www.billcypert.com

7.5 Glossary

Acquisition cost

The cost of an asset before applying sales tax, but after accounting for discounts and incentives.

Active asset

An asset used daily, or for routine business operations.

Alert

A warning that a limit has been achieved, something has changed, or a malfunction has happened. Alerts are regularly generated and overseen by the system management devices and are overseen by the event management process.

Amortization

A method used to prorate an intangible asset's cost over the duration of its useful life.

Assessment

Examination and evaluation to assess if a standard or set of rules is being followed, that records are precise, or that proficiency and viability targets are being met.

Asset

Any resource or capability, including anything that could add to the delivery of a service. Resources incorporate hardware, software entitlements and contracts. An asset record includes financial, contractual and lifecycle data.

Asset accounting

The process of managing and supervising fixed assets through accurate financial recording and reporting.

Asset class

A grouping of assets that share similar characteristics. These classes carry information including useful life, salvage value, account code, category, replacement information, capitalization threshold, depreciation method, and depreciation convention

Asset data

Information used to identify an asset, including location, status, and physical characteristics.

Asset lifecycle

The stages an asset will undergo throughout its useful life, including acquisition, service life, and disposal.

Asset management

A system that manages and maintains an organization's assets throughout their lifecycle. Examples of popular systems include spreadsheets and software solutions.

Asset management software

An application used for the purpose of recording and tracking an asset throughout its lifecycle. In addition, it can provide tools for financial reporting, and often offers the ability to integrate with other software applications like Microsoft Excel.

Asset tag

Labels with an adhesive backing that are used to track a physical asset's location.

Asset tracking

The process of tracking physical assets, which may include scanning technologies and asset tagging.

Attribute

A piece of data about a configuration product. Examples are a name, location, version number, and cost. Attributes of CIs are recorded in the configuration management database (CMDB).

Auditor

A person or firm responsible for performing an official examination of an

189

organization's financial accounts.

Back-out

An exercise that restores a service or other configuration product to a former baseline. Back-out is utilized as a form of remediation when a change or release is unsuccessful.

Balance sheet

The financial statement which summarizes a company's assets, liabilities and shareholder's equity.

Barcode technology

An asset tracking method that utilizes adhesive barcode stickers, each unique and consisting of a group of patterned bars, spaces and/or numbers that, when scanned, are used to identify the item that has been tagged.

Baseline

ITIL *Continual Service Improvement)* (ITIL *Service Transition)* A snapshot that is utilized as a reference point. Numerous snapshots may be taken and recorded after some time but just some will be utilized as baselines. For instance: An ITSM baseline can be utilized as an initial point to gauge the impact of a service enhancement plan

A performance baseline can be utilized to gauge changes in performance over the lifetime of an IT service A configuration baseline can be utilized as a component of a back-out plan to allow the IT infrastructure to be restored to a recognized configuration if a change or release fails.

Bookkeeper

A person responsible for keeping record of an organization's financial activities.

Capital asset

Fixed assets that have the ability to purchase new property for a company.

Capital improvement

Additions or adjustments to property that boost its value, increase useful life, or modify its use.

Capitalization threshold

The minimum cost at which an asset must be reflected in your accounting records. This threshold may be determined by government regulation, or by the standards set forth by your organization.

Capitalized asset

An asset with a total cost that is expensed over future periods, rather than being

191

	expensed completely at the time of procurement or installation.
Category	A named group of products that share something in common. Categories are utilized to group similar products together.
Change	The inclusion, alteration, or disposal of anything that could affect IT services.
Change Advisory Board (CAB)	A group of individuals who support the evaluation, prioritization, approval, and planning of changes. A change advisory board is normally made up of representatives from all areas inside the IT service provider, the business, and third parties such as suppliers.
Change Management	The process in charge of controlling the life cycle of all changes, allowing beneficial changes to be made with least disturbance to IT services.
Change Record	A record containing the details of a change. Every change record documents the life cycle of a single change. A change record is

generated for each request for change.

Change Request

A formal detailed proposal for a change to be made. The term is often misused to mean change record or the change itself.

Classification

The act of allocating a category to something. Classification is utilized to guarantee consistent management and reporting. CIs, incidents, problems, and changes are normally classified.

Closed

The last status in the life cycle of an incident, problem, or change. At the point when the status is closed, no further action is made.

Cloud computing

A type of internet-based computing in which information is stored and used through the internet, rather than saved on a hard drive. Although similar to vendor-hosted software, the two are not the same.

Closure

The act of changing the status of an incident, problem, or change to closed.

Configuration Item (CI)	Any part or another service resource that should be overseen so as to convey an IT service. Data about every configuration product is recorded in a configuration record inside the configuration management system and is maintained all through its life cycle by service asset and configuration management. A CI may be: a **physical entity**, such as a computer or router, a **logical entity**, such as an instance of a database or **Conceptual**, such as a Requisition Service
Configuration Management Database (CMDB)	A database utilized for storing configuration records all through their life cycle. The configuration management system maintains at least one CMDBs. Every CMDB keeps properties of CIs and relationships with other CIs.

Configuration Management System (CMS)

A set of devices, information, and data that is utilized to help service asset and configuration management. The CMS is part of a general service knowledge management and incorporates devices for collecting, storing, managing, updating, analyzing, and presenting information about all configuration products and their relationships. The CMS also incorporates data about incidents, problems, known errors, changes, and releases. It may contain information about staffs, suppliers, locations, business units, clients, and users. The CMS is maintained by service asset and configuration management and is utilized by every IT service management processes.

Configuration Record

A record containing the details of a configuration item. Every configuration record documents the lifecycle of a single configuration item. Configuration records are kept in a configuration management database and maintained as a major aspect of a configuration management system.

Configuration Type

A category that is utilized to classify configuration products. The CI type distinguishes the needed properties and relationships for a configuration record. Common CI types incorporate hardware, document, and user.

Content Service

Customers can opt into the Content Service, anonymously providing software discovery models and processor names that are not normalized, to ServiceNow's internal Content Curation team. This team will then research and update the Software Content Library. At the point when clients decide to opt into the Content Service, they will still have the choice to limit what information is sent to ServiceNow (e.g. homegrown applications will probably be excluded). By having customers share information that is not normalized, we can crowdsource new content and ensure that normalization rates are continuously improved.

| **Continual Service Improvement** | Guarantees that services are aligned with changing business requirements by recognizing and executing enhancements to IT services that help business processes. The performance of the IT service provider is consistently measured and enhancements are made to processes, IT services, and IT infrastructure so as to increase proficiency, efficacy, and cost-effectiveness. |

| **Customer** | Any individual who purchases goods or services. The customer of an IT service provider is the individual or group who characterizes and consents to the service level targets. The term is also sometimes utilized casually to mean user. |

| **Current asset** | Cash or cash equivalents that can be converted into cash within one year. |

| **Depreciation** | A method of allocating a portion of the cost of an asset over the period it can be used. While there are many types of depreciation, the most commonly used is the straight-line method. |

Diagnosis

A phase in the incident and problem life cycles. The reason of diagnosis is to distinguish a workaround for an incident or the main cause of a problem.

Discovery Model

A software discovery model is a 'normalized' version of the discovered software installations that also incorporates properties such as Edition, Version and whether the discovered product is licensable.

Digital asset

An intangible asset that is stored in digital form.

Disposal

Process of selling an asset that has reached the end of its useful life.

Effectiveness

A measure of whether the goals of a process, service, or exercise have been accomplished. An effective process or exercise is one that accomplishes its agreed goals. *See also* Key Performance Indicator.

Efficiency

A measure of whether the appropriate number of assets have been utilized to deliver a process, service, or exercise.

Emergency Change	A change that must be presented at the earliest opportunity, for instance, to settle a major incident or perform a security patch. The change management process usually has a particular procedure for dealing with emergency changes.
Employee Self Service	A module in ServiceNow that enables clients to make demands, see articles, log incidents, and search the knowledge base through a user-friendly site called the Employee Self-Service Portal (ESS Portal).
Event	A change of state that has importance for the management of an IT service or other configuration product. The term is additionally used to mean an alert or warning generated by any IT service, configuration product, or monitoring device.
Exceptions report	A list of discrepancies, or assets not located in the re-inventory process, which is generated by an asset management solution.

Fixed asset

A tangible asset purchased for the intention of long-term use, and that is not consumed or sold during the course of business. Fixed assets cannot be quickly converted into cash, and include land, buildings, and equipment.

Generally Accepted Accounting Principles (GAAP)

Mandatory principles, standards, and procedures used by companies for financial reporting.

Ghost asset

A fixed asset that appears on your financial statement, but is no longer in use because it is missing or has been determined unusable.

Impact

A measure of the effect of an incident, problem, or change on business processes. The impact is regularly dependent on how service levels will be affected. Impact and urgency are used to assign importance.

Inactive asset

An asset not currently used in business operations.

Incident

An unintended interference to an IT service or a decrease in the quality of an IT service. Malfunction of a configuration product that hasn't affected service yet is also an incident.

Income statement

A financial statement detailing a company's revenues and expenses for the purpose of reporting financial performance over the span of the accounting period.

Installed solution

A solution in which data storage servers are located on-site, or in a data warehouse.

Intangible asset

An asset that has no physical presence and cannot be touched. Examples include trademarks and computer software.

Integration

In regard to software, the capability of an asset management solution to successfully combine with another application, such as Excel or QuickBooks, to enhance the efficiency and convenience of the asset tracking process.

Inventory

Items purchased for short-term use, and which do not require close tracking. There are different methods used to perform an inventory, including wall-to-wall, inventory by exception, and inventory by random sample.

Key Performance Indicator (KPI)

A metric that is utilized to help oversee an IT service, process, plan, project, or another exercise. Numerous metrics may be determined, but only the most vital of these are characterized as key performance indicators and utilized to actively manage and report on the process, IT service, or exercise. They ought to be chosen to guarantee that productivity, viability, and cost adequacy are all managed.

Known Error

An issue that has a documented main cause and a workaround. Known errors are generated and managed all through their life cycle by problem management. Development groups or suppliers may also recognize known errors.

License Type

Designates if these are full, outright licenses or upgraded licenses from a previous version or edition
(If the Publisher Part Number (PPN) is known, then License type is not required).

License Metric

The calculation by which compliance is determined for the software title.
The available License metrics are based on which Metric groups are available in an instance.

Major Incident

The highest category of impact for an incident. A major incident results in a major interruption to the business.

Metric

Anything that is measured and reported to help manage a process, IT service, or exercise.

Metric Group

Designates which license metric is used to calculate compliance. A Metric group controls which license metrics are available to be used. It is possible that not all Metric groups will be available in an instance. It is best to check which Metric groups are available, and only choose the license

| **Normalization** | metrics available for the Metric group. The Metric group chosen does not have to correspond to the publisher of the software title.

The normalization process compares the discovered publisher, discovered product, and discovered edition values related to a Discovery Model against the ServiceNow repository of normalized equivalents. Normalized fields are then used to match up entitlements acquired.

| **Policy** | Formally documented management expectations and intentions. Policies are utilized to coordinate choices and to guarantee steady improvement and execution of processes, standards, roles, exercises, IT infrastructure, and so on.

| **Post-implementation Review** | An evaluation that occurs after a change or a project has been executed. It verifies whether the change or project was successful and identifies opportunities for enhancement.

Pre-implementation Review

An evaluation that occurs prior to a change or a project being executed. It verifies the potential impact and identifies opportunities for enhancement.

Priority

A category utilized to identify the relative significance of an incident, issue, or change. Priority is dependent on impact and urgency and is utilized to identify the needed number of times for actions to be taken. For instance, the SLA may state that priority 2 incidents must be settled within 12 hours.

Problem

A cause of one or more incidents. The cause is not always known at the time a problem record is generated. The problem management process is in charge of further investigations.

Property manager

A professional who is responsible for effective, efficient management of assets, including company equipment and materials.

Publisher Part Number (PPN)

The part number of the software title for which rights were obtained. The PPN is the simplest way to ensure success when importing/generating software entitlements. If a part number is not available, the Publisher, Product, Version and Edition fields must be populated. Depending on how the software is acquired, it may be necessary to populate the Platform and Language as well.

QR code

A type of barcode that is used to identify an item and store information. The code is comprised of black squares which are arranged in a grid.

RACI

A model utilized to help characterize roles and obligations. RACI stands for responsible, accountable, consulted, and informed.

Radio Frequency Identification (RFID) technology

Technology used to identify objects by utilizing data-encoded RFID tags, which are then captured by a reader through radio waves. Unlike barcode technology, RFID can be used to identify objects that are out of vision.

Reconciliation   The process of comparing asset information in your records with the current status of the assets and correcting mistakes or deficiencies in order to keep asset records up to date

Release   At least one change in IT service that is built, tested and deployed together. A single release may incorporate changes to hardware, software, documentation, process, and other parts.

Request for Change   A formal detailed proposal for a change to be made. The term is regularly misused to mean change record or the change itself.

Restore   Making a move to restore an IT service to the clients after fixing and recovery from an incident. This is the main goal of incident management.

Risk   A possible event that could cause harm or loss or influence the capacity to accomplish targets. A risk is estimated by the likelihood of a threat, the vulnerability of the resource for that danger, and the effect it would have in the event that it happened.

Role

A set of responsibilities, exercises, and authorizations allocated to an individual or group. A role is characterized by a procedure or function. One individual or group may have various roles. For instance, a single individual may do the job of a configuration manager and change manager.

Root Cause

The fundamental or unique reason for an incident or issue.

Root Cause Analysis (RCA)

An exercise that recognizes the main cause of an incident or issue. Root cause analysis normally focuses on IT infrastructure failures.

Scanning technology

Used in conjunction with barcode or RFID tags, scanners simplify the asset tracking process and maximize efficiency

Sensitive asset

An asset that has potential to be impacted by external factors. A sensitive asset can fall into one of the following categories: interest-sensitive or theft-sensitive.

Service	A way of providing value to the clients by enabling the results that clients want to accomplish without the ownership of specific expenses or risks.
Service Desk	The single point of contact between the service provider and the customers. A regular service desk oversees incidents and service requests and additionally takes care of communication with the customer.
Service Level	Measured and reported accomplishment against one or more service level objectives.
Service Level Agreement (SLA)	A contract between an IT service provider and a client. A service level agreement explains the IT service; documents, service level objectives and specifies the obligations of the IT service provider and the client.
Service Request	A formal request from a customer for something to be provided, for instance, a request for information or guidance; to reset a password, or to set up a workstation for a new user.

Software Asset Management Content Library	The Content Library allows companies to harness: Normalization rules to standardize software installations in the ServiceNow® CMDB Publishers, products, and more to standardize data and eliminate many of the manual actions in the software asset management lifecycle Pre-built publisher part number definitions and discovery maps to automatically relate acquired software to the accurate software installations Processor definitions to understand accurate processor names so that the suitable processor core factors can be applied amid reconciliation
Software as a Service (SaaS)	An Internet Based Software distribution model in which an Organization subscribes to and accesses an application through the internet.
Software Entitlement	Software entitlements ensure that the rights defined in a Software License are being used by the right users/devices, in the right places, at the right time. Software entitlements

define license metric details and are allocated to software models. To successfully generate a Software Entitlement, Publisher and Product details are needed as a minimum.

Software Installation

Discovery tools discover the software underline installed on a device on a company's network domain. (e.g. SN Discovery, Microsoft SCCM). Software installation information is often difficult to understand and needs normalization.

Software License

Grants a client the right to use a specific piece of software. It contains a set of terms and conditions that define to what extent you may legally use that software.

Software Model

Software Models are version specific and represent what a company has acquired. They are generated for all installed software products inside a company and are used to tie software installations (software being used) with entitlements (software owned). A Software Model consists of Publisher, Product, Version,

	Edition, Platform and Language
Software Product	A software title that is version agnostic, e.g. Office, Captivate
Spreadsheet	Created using applications like Microsoft's Excel or Google Drive, companies often use spreadsheets to track assets as an alternative to asset management software. Though a cheaper option, there are many flaws and risks associated with using spreadsheets to manage assets.
Stakeholder	An individual who has an interest in a company, project, or IT service. Stakeholders may be interested in the exercises, goals, assets, or deliverables. Stakeholders may incorporate clients, partners, staff member, shareholders, owners, or others.
Tangible asset	An asset with a Physical presence that can be touched.
Useful life (service life)	An estimate of the duration of time that an asset is forecasted to be in service

	for the reason it was purchased.
User	An individual who makes use of the IT service on a daily basis. Users are different from customers, as some customers do not use the IT service directly.
Vendor hosted software	Software that is installed and accessed from a remote server by a third-party vendor.
Workaround	Decreasing or eliminating the effect of an incident or issue which doesn't have a solution yet, for instance, by rebooting a failed configuration product. Workarounds for issues are documented in known error records. Workarounds for incidents that don't have related problem records are documented in the incident record.
Zombie asset	A capitalized fixed asset that is still in use, but not reflected in account records.

Page Intentionally left blank to preserve
section layout.

www.billcypert.com

7.6 SN SAM Orlando New Features & Updates

7.6.1 SAM Vulnerability Assessment

When thinking about the security of your environment, software must be considered a major factor. Are you sure you understand the exact position of ALL software on your network? If you answered yes, then I would be shocked. Think about shadow IT spend on software, blacklisted software, BYOD devices that have their own software and how this presents increased risk to your organization.

This is where the, new in Orlando, SAM Vulnerability Assessment feature comes to the rescue. Ok rescue is a strong word, how about this new feature seeks to help you with the real issue in your organization? If you have Security and Software Asset on the same page, then your ability to find and remediate software vulnerabilities is greatly enhanced. We have always had the ability to run workflows in SAM and in VR (vulnerability response) but never before have we had such a seamless connection between the two areas. This in turn should lead to better operations in a more secure environment.

The National Vulnerability Database (NVD) contains information regarding software versions that have known vulnerabilities. SAM, in Orlando, now leverages the NVD to enhance the identification of potential issues (vulnerabilities). Combine this with the ever-growing Content Library provided by ServiceNow SAM and it becomes a very powerful weapon in the normalization of application discovery models. Once we have normalization, then we find it much easier to get true visibility of our vulnerabilities and subsequently remediate them.

7.6.2 SaaS License Connections

One of the issues we have faced in the world of software management is how we could accurately measure SaaS applications. Many organizations rely only on what the vendor is telling them via their vendor dashboard. Unfortunately, this presents a conflict of interest in that the SaaS company is not likely to be consistently showing you where you could achieve the best savings. This is where the SaaS License Connections comes into play. ServiceNow has been tracking certain SaaS based assets for years, but now we are starting to really see more maturity in this space. A non-comprehensive list of SaaS apps tracked in Orlando is:

Adobe Creative Cloud

Box

DropBox

DocuSign

G-Suite

Jira

Office 365

SalesForce Sales Cloud

SalesForce Service Cloud

WebEx

Zoom

This list is non-comprehensive because quite frankly you can leverage Flow designer & Integration Hub to pull together a low-code integration with almost every SaaS provider assuming they have an open API.

7.6.3 SaaS License Management (enhanced)

Beginning in the New York release, SaaS License Management was available to SAM customers. The purpose of SaaS License Management is to give you the ability to detect, analyze and optimize SaaS licensing across the organization.

In Orlando this feature has been enhanced to specifically provide additional features for WebEx and Jira. Now we can get much deeper from within ServiceNow in terms of usage and cost for both WebEx and Jira.

Webex

Increased visibility for Cisco WebEx Meetings now reveals not only usage data but also variance of licenses against the purchased allocations. This visibility will give you the best data for making reclamation, additional purchase and audit defense moves. Last hosted meeting information helps determine which licensees are stale. Of course, this is variable from organization to organization. Personally, I have most often seen org's that issue a warning at 60 days and removal in 90 days. However, I have seen some go to 30/60, especially when approaching contract renewals or audits.

Jira

Jira is handled in a similar way to WebEx, but rather than meeting date as a key factor, we most often look to issue creation or other activities in the audit log. Again, like in WebEx, you will make your own warning/removal thresholds.

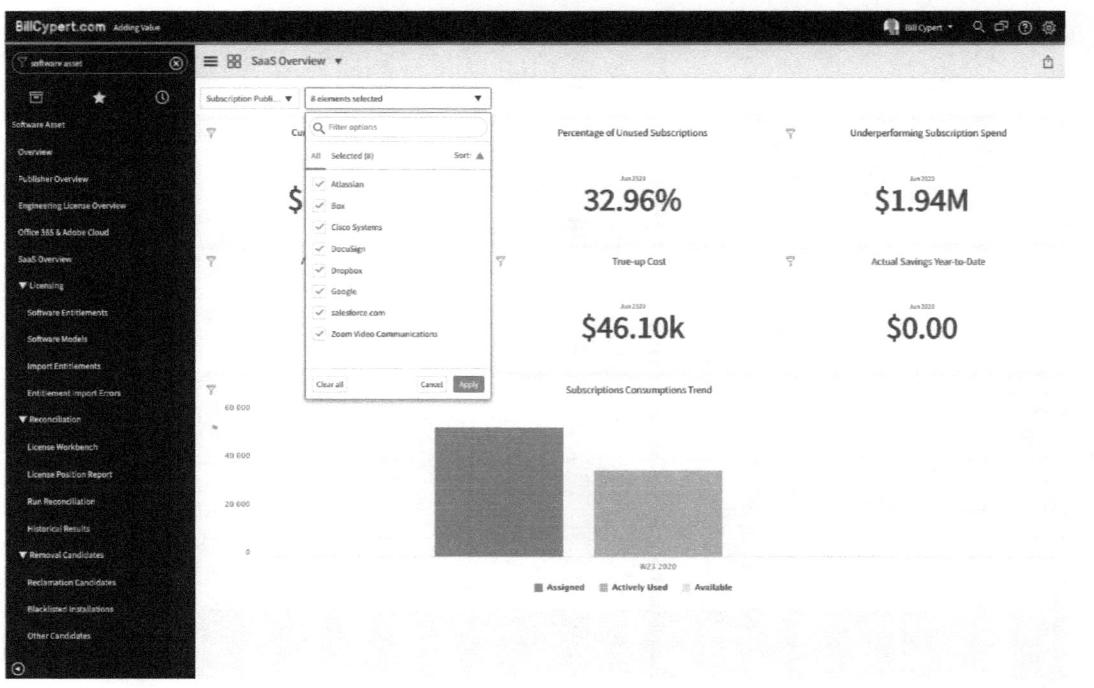

BillCypert.com Adding Value
Bill Cypert
SaaS Overview
software asset
Software Asset
Overview
Publisher Overview
Engineering License Overview
Office 365 & Adobe Cloud
SaaS Overview
Licensing
Software Entitlements
Software Models
Import Entitlements
Entitlement Import Errors
Reconciliation
License Workbench
License Position Report
Run Reconciliation
Historical Results
Removal Candidates
Reclamation Candidates
Blacklisted Installations
Other Candidates
Subscription Publi...
8 elements selected
Filter options
All   Selected (8)   Sort:
Atlassian
Box
Cisco Systems
DocuSign
Dropbox
Google
salesforce.com
Zoom Video Communications
Clear all   Cancel   Apply
Percentage of Unused Subscriptions
Jun 2020
32.96%
Underperforming Subscription Spend
Jun 2020
$1.94M
True-up Cost
Jun 2020
$46.10k
Actual Savings Year-to-Date
Jun 2020
$0.00
Subscriptions Consumptions Trend
60 000
40 000
20 000
0
W23 2020
Assigned   Actively Used   Available

7.6.4 Engineering License Manager

The proliferation of specialty software has presented a major problem for those of us trying to get a handle on our software positions. This is a major cost and security risk for the organization. Engineering License Manager is designed to address exactly these issues by providing visibility into areas that without it would be difficult to see.

Engineering License Manager (ELM) is tied directly to OpenLM which has a ton of benefits especially in the area of engineering licenses. The beauty here is that you, now with the ELM, tie into additional license management servers and thereby have more good data automatically fed into the SN SAM system. Inline with the overall goals of SN SAM you get information on what is owned, how it is being used which translates into opportunities to reduce associated costs.

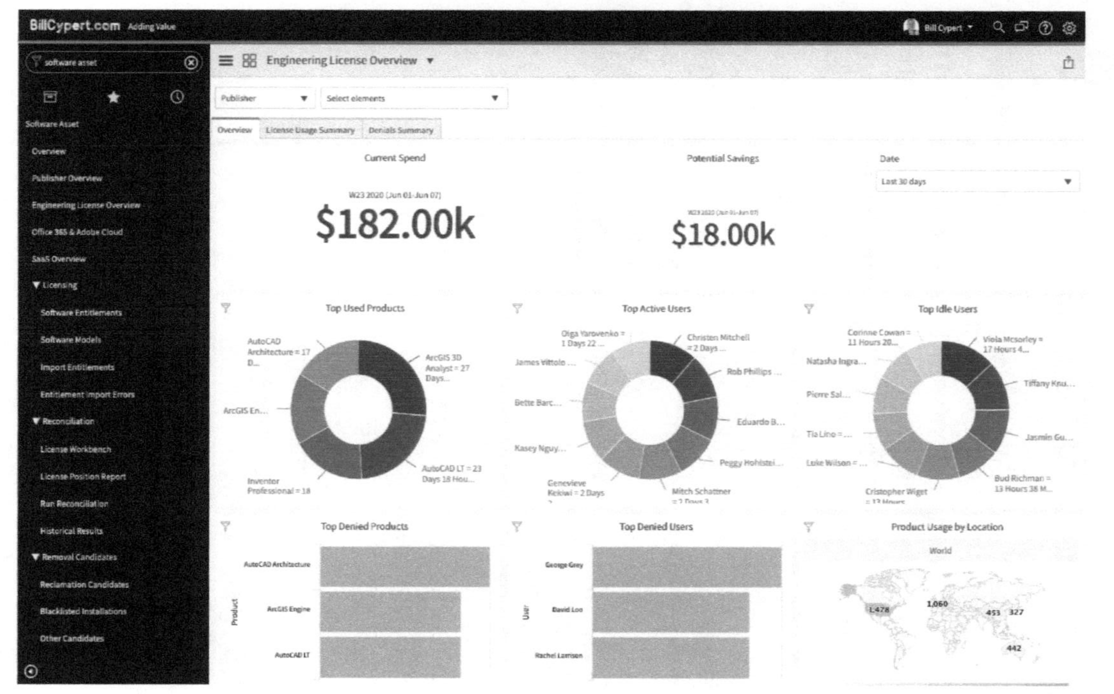

BillCypert.com Adding Value
Bill Cypert
software asset
Engineering License Overview
Software Asset
Overview
Publisher Overview
Engineering License Overview
Office 365 & Adobe Cloud
SaaS Overview
Licensing
Software Entitlements
Software Models
Import Entitlements
Entitlement Import Errors
Reconciliation
License Workbench
License Position Report
Run Reconciliation
Historical Results
Removal Candidates
Reclamation Candidates
Blacklisted Installations
Other Candidates
Publisher
Select elements
Overview
License Usage Summary
Denials Summary
Current Spend
W23 2020 (Jun 01-Jun 07)
$182.00k
Potential Savings
W23 2020 (Jun 01-Jun 07)
$18.00k
Date
Last 30 days
Top Used Products
AutoCAD Architecture = 17 D...
ArcGIS 3D Analyst = 27 Days...
ArcGIS En...
AutoCAD LT = 23 Days 18 Hou...
Inventor Professional = 18
Top Active Users
Olga Yarovenko = 1 Days 22 ...
Christen Mitchell = 2 Days ...
James Vittolo ...
Rob Phillips ...
Bette Barc...
Eduardo B...
Kasey Nguy...
Peggy Hohlstei...
Genevieve Rickiwi = 2 Days
Mitch Schatzner = 2 Days 2
Top Idle Users
Corinne Cowan = 11 Hours 20...
Viola Mcsorley = 17 Hours 4...
Natasha Ingra...
Tiffany Knu...
Pierre Sal...
Tia Lino = ...
Jasmin Gu...
Luke Wilson = ...
Bud Richman = 13 Hours 38 M...
Cristopher Wiget = 13 Hours
Top Denied Products
Product
AutoCAD Architecture
ArcGIS Engine
AutoCAD LT
Top Denied Users
User
George Grey
David Loo
Rachel Larrison
Product Usage by Location
World
1,478
1,060
453
327
442

7.6.5 Software Maintenance

In the world of software, specifically software sales, we know that one of the most profitable parts of deals is the maintenance. The beauty here from the vendor side is that it is recurring revenue without much cost to support. This "beauty" from the vendor side is not always "beauty" from the customer point of view.

Often organizations choose the path of least resistance by just renewing maintenance contracts without much thought. What happens when you do not realize that much of the maintenance you are paying for is covering software that is not being utilized? This has a compounding effect on the overall cost of software vs the value it brings to your organization.

Leveraging SN Software Maintenance allows you to quickly ascertain your current position and how that translates into what Software Maintenance you actually need from your vendors. You can see how useful this information is going into a renewal period, not to mention just having more information for your TCO calculations.

7.6.6 Automatic license metric assignments

License metric intelligence and the Content Library provide an automated way to assign licensing metrics to your assets. This reduces the time you must dedicate to researching publishers, which thereby yields faster and more accurate license positions.

7.6.7 Office 365 Publisher Pack (enhancements)

An improvement brought to us in the SN SAM Orlando version is the ability to track Office 365 reserve licenses. This feature allows us to reserve subscriptions for part or all of the contract period. Also, we now have increased insight into things like total subscription count and we are better positioned for audits. No longer do we need to depend on the vendor for true-up positioning, now we can walk into the audit with confidence.

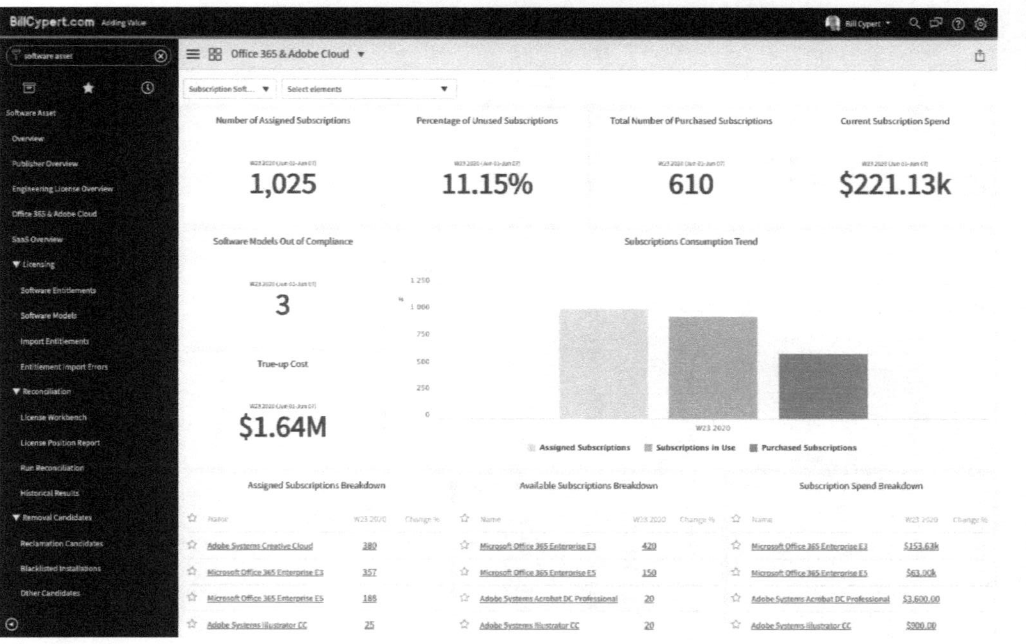

Assigned Subscriptions Breakdown

Name	W23 2020	Change %
Adobe Systems Creative Cloud	380	
Microsoft Office 365 Enterprise E3	357	
Microsoft Office 365 Enterprise E5	185	
Adobe Systems Illustrator CC	25	

Available Subscriptions Breakdown

Name	W23 2020	Change %
Microsoft Office 365 Enterprise E3	420	
Microsoft Office 365 Enterprise E5	150	
Adobe Systems Acrobat DC Professional	20	
Adobe Systems Illustrator CC	20	

Subscription Spend Breakdown

Name	W23 2020	Change %
Microsoft Office 365 Enterprise E3	$153.63k	
Microsoft Office 365 Enterprise E5	$63.00k	
Adobe Systems Acrobat DC Professional	$3,600.00	
Adobe Systems Illustrator CC	$300.00	

7.6.8 Oracle Infrastructure Report

Oracle audits require database versions, CPU counts, other hardware information, virtual machine / container information for each and every database instance. This is pain to collect, but the good news is that SN SAM Orlando version will help get you down the road with the Oracle Infrastructure Report.

7.6.9 Entitlement import enhancements

Entitlements have always been an area we need to remain hyper-focused on to be success with SAM. ServiceNow made several important Entitlement Import Enhancements in the Orlando version of the software. Here are some of the specific use cases:

Importing Contracts

Importing Custom Defined Fields

References to Existing Contracts

7.7 Thank you

I appreciate you taking time to share my passion for Software Asset Management. You, the consumer of this information are the ones who made this book possible and for that I **thank you**.

Honestly it was my intention to end the book with the Glossary, but how could I end this labor of love with "Zombie Asset"?

In all seriousness, I do sincerely thank you and look forward to your comments.   Please feel free to reach out to me and / or leave your comments on my blog at billcypert.com.

Bill Cypert
bill@billcypert.com